THE
CONTRACTOR
LIFESTYLE

How to Be Highly Sought After By Employers and Develop a Career that's Immune to Layoffs and Recessions

GEORGE VERDOLAGA

Visit the author's website at **www.georgeverdolaga.com**

ISBN: 978-0-9865636-1-4

Cover design by Greg Lam

Copyediting, proofreading, indexing and interior design by Ted Morrison

Other useful resources from George Verdolaga

Visit **www.sittingprettycourse.com** to discover the most powerful and effective way to find work:

- ***Discover the back door*** *to finding a job, and how to use it to beat the competition*

- ***Uncover the key decision-makers*** *who have the power to offer you a job on the spot*

- ***Understand why mass-mailing resumes*** *to human resource departments or going through a third-party recruiter doesn't work*

- ***Find out the techniques*** *that successful people use to turn interviews into job offers*

- ***Learn how to get glowing reviews*** *from your former bosses and co-workers*

- ***Master the one habit*** *that will ensure that you'll never be out of work, and have employers running after you instead*

To start closing the gap between your current reality and the abundant and purposeful life you want to lead go to **www.personalandcareerplanner.com**

- ***Get your career and your personal life back on track***

- ***Figure out what you want*** *and what you need to do to get to where you want*

- ***Inventory your strengths and weaknesses*** *and find out what type of working environment best suits you*

- ***Understand your natural preferences*** *and learn to use these to your advantage in your work and personal life*

- ***Uncover your special gifts*** *and decide how to use them to make other people's lives better*

Subscribe to the BULLETPROOF Newsletter, a powerful source of ideas to help you get ahead in your career and in life, at **www.georgeverdolaga.com/newsletter**

ACKNOWLEDGEMENTS

I am eternally grateful first and foremost to my wife, for standing patiently by my side through all those early mornings when she had to endure a noisy alarm clock to help me wake me up to another day of writing. None of this would have been possible without her unconditional love and support and also her own wisdom and experience.

I am also thankful for my wonderful parents, whose prayers and constant encouragement have enabled me to continuously pursue my dreams and goals. They have always been around to offer me guidance and strength, and they have never failed to believe in me. I dedicate this book to them.

I'm also grateful to my production team: Greg Lam, without whom the technical aspects of the website and audio production would not have been possible—thank you for helping me bring my work to the digital age, my friend. And Ted Morrison, my editor, whose utter generosity, refreshing cooperation and invaluable experience have helped to make this book and my home study course (Sitting Pretty: The Powerful And Effective Way To Find A Job That's Right For You Right Now) a reality.

I also thank my friends who lent me their time and energy to help make this book come to fruition.

You all know who you are and I truly appreciate your contribution to this project.

And finally to our Creator for slowly revealing the true purpose of my life and tying all the pieces together and helping me discover and use all my special gifts for the benefit of others—finally it all makes sense.

TABLE OF CONTENTS

INTRODUCTION

Are you tired of the same old daily grind? Do you wonder if you'd be happier doing something else? Does your work make you feel weary or bitter? Is your job under threat from changes in the industry or workplace? Are you perfectly happy at your current job but wondering how to boost your performance or whether there might not be something better elsewhere?

Hi there. My name's George Verdolaga, and I wrote this book for you.

This book is intended for people who feel they've hit a career dead end. It's for people who are demoralized by mind games or a scarcity mentality at work.

This book is for people afraid of losing their jobs as a result of a takeover or due to downsizing. This book is also meant for people who've been unhappy with what they're doing and are bravely contemplating leaving the comfort and security of a paying job for something more fulfilling.

This book is also intended for people who still want to make a genuine difference in the world through their work, to be inspired to come to work every day, and to have people recognize them as valuable resources in their chosen fields.

To help you on your journey to career and financial independence, I've included links to additional resources near the end of almost every chapter. These links outline very specific job finding strategies and amplify points made in this book. Some of the links help keep you up to date on the latest developments, or keep you apprised of new or upcoming courses.

I've also referred to a useful workbook resource to assist you in moving forward, in case you find yourself stuck and need to figure out what your next steps should be to get moving again.

It all boils down to a radical idea: As a 21st century employee, you need to think like a contractor and focus on delivering a stellar performance and bringing more value to the table every single day, rather than holding on to your job at all costs.

It also means looking at your career as a business and your boss and co-workers as valuable "clients", who require your expertise to solve their problems, and whose trust and approval you need to win every single day. It also requires that you develop solid relationships within—and outside your company—in order to ensure that you're never out of work.

Companies, on the other hand need to look out for their employees better and be more positive and inspiring places to work. Unhappy and unmotivated employees are simply going to be a drain on productivity and morale, and won't be helpful in enabling companies to be more competitive in the marketplace.

This book will help you understand how different jobs are in the current century compared to the previous one, and why "job security" is an idea that is no longer sustainable. You will come to understand that job instability is the new 21st century reality. And you'll also learn why that doesn't have to be a worry for you.

You'll see that economies worldwide go through a continuous cycle of boom and bust, making your company stronger or taking it down, along with you and your coworkers. You'll see how things can change very rapidly, and how your perfect company could suddenly become hellish with a relatively minor change in personnel.

You'll also see the 21st century corporate landscape at a time when foreign competition is right at your company's doorstep ready to eat its lunch, and yours, with cheaper products and labor. You'll learn how to ride this wave of uncertainty and acquire the necessary survival skills to help you become exactly the kind of employee more companies need.

Whether you're currently employed or between jobs, you can understand how companies decide who to keep or let go when they're laying people off.

You'll get insights into how to avoid lethal office politics that will hurt your career. You'll understand the importance of building strong ties, especially with the key decision-makers in your workplace who can help you to get ahead. You'll also learn how to obtain and use information to enable you to enjoy a thriving career.

You will also learn why it pays to never burn bridges and why it's a good idea to stay on good terms with ex-bosses and keep in touch with former coworkers. This book will also highlight how important being at the top of your game is to the longevity and success of your career.

You'll be interested to discover how leaving your current workplace can be a win-win situation for you and your current employer, and why you should constantly be on the lookout for great career opportunities. More importantly, you'll learn how change can be good, and how radical change may be what's necessary for you to get ahead. **You'll learn how to adopt a contractor mindset** and look at your job as an assignment, rather than a lifetime commitment. This will help enable you to avoid getting the rug pulled out from under you.

For companies and managers, this book is a wake-up call to understand how to use motivators other than pay such as recognition, feedback, mentoring and training to hold on to good employees and help them rise up the company ladder. **It's an opportunity for employers to find ways to win the hearts and minds of their people**, who are becoming increasingly hard to keep.

Companies can learn how to get their employees to buy into the corporate mission, vision and values, to the benefit of the customers they serve and also their immediate communities. They'll also understand how being people-centered enables them to thrive.

Why did I write this book? What made me an authority on how to find work easily? Simple: I've lived it. And I found out by trial and error, over a long and sometimes painful span of years, the things I've gathered together and written down here.

I started my career as an employee for several firms before finally becoming my own boss. I feel fortunate to be working for myself in a profession that I love. It can be that way for you too, or for anybody. And best of all, you don't have to stumble on the answers the way I did. It is my hope that you can learn the lessons the easy way: by reading and following the advice in this book.

Sincerely,

George Verdolaga

CHAPTER 1
LIFETIME CONTRACTS ARE OVER

Jobs as we know them are going the way of the dinosaur

The job as we know it, or rather knew it, is a product of the industrial revolution. Prior to factories and assembly lines, people essentially worked in a single profession their whole lives. If you were a blacksmith or a weaver, that was what you did from the time you started in that profession, possibly in your early teens, until you were too old to continue. Goods were produced laboriously by craftspeople, one item at a time. Often the quality was inconsistent and everyone basically was self-employed.

Business ebbed and flowed with the seasons, and the market for goods was not as widespread as it is today. Economies were not as interconnected as they are now. One might not know what to expect in terms of income from week to week, and there wasn't any such thing as social security or unemployment insurance.

The industrial revolution gave rise to a new work order. Goods once produced in small shops by skilled owner-operators could now be made in factories more cheaply and quickly using comparatively unskilled labor. Long years of apprenticeship were no longer required, as mechanized production became standardized.

A new generation emerged that consisted of people who were no longer confined to their parents' trades but who went to work each day at an office or on an assembly line. New opportunities also arose for a more educated class of support and administrative workers such as secretaries, clerks and managers. These non-production employees became known as "white collar" workers, while those who stayed on the production lines were eventually referred to as "blue collar" workers.

Just as stores selling tools and clothing to miners sprung up around gold rush towns, many new businesses opened to service the needs of factory and office workers. Cities boomed, and people got used to working at the same factory or office in perpetuity.

Competition between companies was strong, but there was plenty of room in the marketplace. "Outsourcing" wasn't even a word back then. Continuous employment brought regular wages, and many families became more financially stable, and better off, as a result of the emergence of an urban-based middle class.

Life in the 19th century was initially pretty harsh for an industrial worker. Children as young as five or six might work as much as fourteen hours per day in a factory. A work week might be as long as a hundred hours, and the average was around sixty. The concept of weekends didn't even exist back then.

Under the influence of reformers, enlightened industrialists and trade unions, work conditions became much better, and working hours shorter. Instead of working seasonally, people could now work the whole year round and earn a steady—as opposed to erratic—income. It was a level of security that made it possible for working people to save money and plan ahead.

In the eyes of many employees back then, long hours and harsh working conditions were compensated for by the prospect of regular full-time work and pay in a factory or office that would provide them with employment for pretty much their whole lives. It was a level of job security that no one had ever had before, and that very few have today.

Instability is the new reality

What a difference a century makes. **The days when people expected to work their whole lives in one place are definitely over.** In the current Information

Age, companies have the power to hire and fire workers more or less at will.

The Japanese, champions of lifetime employment and unwavering loyalty to employees (and vice versa), witnessed mass layoffs during the economic stagnation of the 1990s. Many other workers worldwide have also seen their dreams fall by the wayside as a result of cuts brought on by recession, technological change, or other factors.

Even government agencies, once considered the bastion of secure employment, no longer guarantee lifetime jobs: "James" worked in the maintenance department of a government hospital for more than a decade, secure in the knowledge that he could expect to work there pretty much all his life. Like his fellow "lifers" he was keeping the hospital patients safe and infection-free for close to $18 per hour, which was a decent government wage. The work might not have been "cushy," but it was a comfortable and secure existence.

And then one day, the government announced that it was going to outsource hospital housekeeping functions to save $13 million a year. The contract went to Aramark, a large company providing contract building maintenance, housekeeping and food services. James had a choice between doing the same job for half his former wage if he worked for Aramark, or going to look for another job.

He was in his mid-30s, fortunately, and was young enough to find a position elsewhere. But many of his older colleagues, closer to retirement or unwilling to retrain, didn't fare as well. They became quite bitter at having been deprived of jobs they thought they had for life.

Lifetime employment is a vanishing concept. In the increasingly-rare companies that still offer jobs for life, and in nations where law makes it difficult to release workers from employment, you'll often see employees simply marking time and collecting paychecks, disconnected from what they're doing, and from what the company is trying to accomplish. Their careers may have stagnated to the point where they are unemployable outside their customary niche. They may even be unhappy, though not so unhappy that they'll sacrifice security and move elsewhere for more satisfying work. So people cling to the illusion of "job security," hoping to be able to keep their jobs until they retire.

A company doesn't exist to make people comfortable and happy at all costs. It exists to deliver great products and services and do this at a profit, while hopefully treating employees fairly and decently in the process. The bargain used to be that a company offered employees regular pay, hours, and benefits, in return for a certain amount of output over a certain amount of time each week.

In the wake of successive recessions and increased global competition, the playing field has tilted toward employers, giving them free rein to pull the rug from underneath people if required. "Job security" has all but disappeared.

But while a company has to be flexible enough to hire and fire almost at will, it also needs to provide a minimal amount of security and reasonable wages and benefits in order to be a place where people want to work. **Companies have to provide challenges, keep people interested, and keep them connected to the corporate mission.** They also need to truly engage people's hearts and minds in the process and not simply give the idea lip service.

Some places are better at this than others. Although getting paid well is a huge motivator, people will stay at a company, despite lower pay, if it's in alignment with their own values and beliefs. People also want to develop their careers, and providing them with training is a great way for them to feel that they're continuously growing as professionals.

What this means to employees is that if you find yourself getting too comfortable, if the job doesn't match your values, or if you are no longer challenged, you need to get out of your comfort zone and seek fresh opportunities within the company to see how you can develop professionally and increase your pay.

If these outcomes aren't possible within your own company, look to other firms outside your current one to see who can provide you with these opportunities. **Change can be good, and radical change may be just what you need.**

The world is evolving very quickly

More people now find themselves in inherently unstable situations. These days, though, it's not a person in the same city who is competing for a job you want; it might be someone halfway around the world who has the same skill set as you but is willing to work for a fraction of your wage.

Jobs increasingly are becoming less location-based. What can't be made by machines can often be produced by someone else in the world, where raw materials cost less, tax rates are lower, or regulation is more lax. Knowledge- and information-based work can now be performed or delivered these days over a broadband connection, reducing the need for office space and furniture, making these lean and mean companies more competitive and therefore, cheaper. They're the ones who are about to eat your company's lunch.

Even surgeons are now perfecting techniques for operating remotely on patients. Long distance or "tele-surgeries" over virtual private networks (VPN) or fiber optic links are becoming increasingly common. And technology will continue to evolve. It won't be long before robots with artificial intelligence will replace human beings to do much of the work that we still currently do.

Boom-and-bust cycles will help to ensure that nothing is certain

If you've been in the workforce long enough, you might have gone through half a dozen recessions. And if you've been on Earth for more than 50 years, you might have even seen a dozen or more. Each recession sees the loss of thousands of positions that will never be reopened or refilled as a result of the creation and destruction of not just companies, but whole industries.

These cyclical boom-and-bust cycles have continued to bring us moments of prosperity and hardship. Just as the world economy was recovering from the Asian currency crisis of 1997 for instance, the dot-com bubble finally burst in 2000, creating a mild recession and unemployment, particularly in the high tech sector. After less than a decade of recovery, we have had the subprime mortgage crisis of 2008, which has yet to run its course.

It's safe to say that we'll continue to see and feel the effects of these up-and-down economic roller coaster rides much more quickly than we ever did in the past as the global economy becomes more interconnected as time passes.

Holding on to company employees is becoming harder and harder each day. Corporations periodically have to cut back on staff, especially if their profit margins are threatened. Regardless of how reliable or faithful those employees have been, company owners and managers have slowly come to realize that it's no longer realistic, or even possible, to offer lifetime employment to anyone, especially if the firm's very survival is at stake. And it isn't just factory floor and manual labor jobs that are at risk. Even management positions are in constant danger of being eliminated.

As more and more companies no longer offer jobs for life, employees are learning to look at options outside their company in order to mitigate any risks to their careers. And companies that can't make themselves attractive or inspiring places to work, in the meantime, experience constant "churn" (i.e. employee turnover).

This contributes to an unhappy working environment and to the inherent instability which causes the churn in the first place. Unfortunately, not all companies are quick to fix this situation, especially if it doesn't sufficiently disrupt the bottom line.

The picture may look grim for workers. Their jobs are threatened by cheaper overseas labor, encroaching technology, and the ever-present possibility of economic downturn. **But there are ways to avoid, and even take advantage of, the current climate of instability.**

No matter whether or not you love what you do, you can't really afford to fall in love with a single company. A number of firms will only keep you for as long as it works for them financially, being profit-driven enterprises first and foremost. It isn't "disloyal" to equip yourself with the tools to make a success of yourself outside your current firm, just as it's no longer regarded as disloyal for a company to dump hundreds, or even thousands, of employees in response to pressure on their profit margins. **In fact, these same survival skills will help turn you into exactly the kind of employee more companies need.**

Reimagine your job as a temporary assignment

So if jobs as we know them are slowly disappearing and companies are no longer expanding their work-forces, how can people protect themselves? The first step is to recognize the fundamental reality: **You have to accept that you probably won't spend your whole career in just one company.**

You will most likely work in a series of companies or industries out of choice, or as a result of some unforeseen event. More than a few investment bankers and stockbrokers, for instance, had to re-invent themselves or find a way to ride out the storm, as a result of the 2008 subprime mortgage crisis. Realtors and mortgage brokers had to get second jobs or switch careers immediately following the debacle, as the housing market slowed to a halt.

You may not be able to get all the training or experience that you need from one company. You may need to learn on your own, on your own dime and on your own time. Or you may have to move to a different company just to keep on learning and growing and continue moving forward.

This may sound like hard work. But the reality is that this is what's necessary in the modern workplace. And besides, you want to move onward and upward, to better pay and perks, don't you? So if you feel that you're stagnating in one company, you must consider your options not only within, but outside of the company. Otherwise, you may find yourself getting blindsided during tough economic periods.

If you're a valuable and direct contributor to the company's bottom line, then your job is most likely safe. But if you feel that you're just a cog in the wheel, buried somewhere in the middle where no one knows what you're doing and that you even exist, then you need to write your own insurance policy. You need to be independent, not relying on just one employer for your career stability.

You need to stay on your toes: **While you're working for someone, you must continue to bring value to the table, or do work that directly contributes to the company's bottom line in order to get paid well and keep your job**. That often means seeking higher education and continuous upgrading of your knowledge and skills. People who have survived the cycle of layoffs and hiring, and thrived, no longer just wear one or two hats, they wear many.

If you don't pick up any new skills or knowledge, the company may decide not to keep you, especially when they have to choose who to lay off. When companies have to be lean and mean, they also have to make sure that the people they retain can pick up the slack. That also means more work for those who are left. You'll likely be expected to contribute more value than ever before if you want to stay continuously employed. While it may seem like a huge burden, it's also an opportunity to learn, to grow, and to show the boss what you're capable of.

Here are four important things to keep in mind:

1. Your relationship with your company is primarily a business arrangement, no matter how much you love to be there.

2. Things can change quickly, as you may have experienced or seen from the experience of others who've been laid off unexpectedly.

3. YOU need to look out for your career 24/7, because no one else will.

4. You should seriously consider opportunities in and outside your workplace. It might be good for you and your employer to part ways. After all, you can always get back together later.

Sometimes the best thing you can do is leave

We've touched on one of the best reasons to leave your job: to gain even more experience and education. The idea that gaining those two things will help further your career should be plain. **But how can your departure work to improve things for your old workplace?** Here's an example:

Mario Litonjua currently works at a telecommunications company as the head of their Broadband & Landline Marketing Group. Early in his career, he struggled with the decision to leave Comark International, a family-owned consumer goods company where he was happy and doing well, in order to pursue other opportunities to better himself. Mario had reached a point where he felt that he wasn't learning anything new and was stagnating.

He approached the owners of the company and explained his situation, saying that he felt that he needed to move to a larger company where he could grow professionally. In addition to accepting a job offer from the RFM Corporation, a much larger food and beverage company, Mario enrolled at a top business school, taking night classes to sharpen his marketing and management skills.

But he didn't turn his back on the past. Along the way he kept in touch with his former employer, and even gave them advice on their marketing campaigns. After spending several years at RFM, he eventually decided to rejoin his former company, as he found it a really good experience to work for them.

Mario's experience and training paid huge dividends for Comark when he returned. They were able to greatly benefit from the wisdom and insights that he picked up working for a much larger company that had a more diversified product line and deeper and sophisticated marketing experience. His departure ended up being a win-win situation for both Mario and this family-owned business once they resumed their working relationship.

You never know where you're going to end up, and you might even be called back to work again for an old employer. By going out into the world to learn more and gain experience, you get a chance to contribute a lot more than had you been content with staying in the same place. **More often than not if you return to an old company with new skills after some time working elsewhere you'll get promoted and paid even more.**

It's easier to get taken for granted and passed over for promotion if you work for several years at one company. Businesses sometimes have a strange way of hiring people from outside their own talent pool and abruptly giving them supervisory roles, even though they may have perfectly suited people within the company. Sometimes, a whiff of "fresh air" and a new jolt of energy is enough for companies to hand out coveted positions to outsiders.

So why not take the opportunity to be that outsider for a while, and get invited back at a higher salary and with a fancier title? To be at the top of your game, you need to be near the cutting edge of your profession and your industry. And doing that might mean changing companies.

Never burn your bridges. When you choose to leave, meet with your boss and explain that your leaving has to do with you taking care of yourself for a while, in order to increase your value as a professional. Companies will often understand if you have to explore other options because you're no longer feeling challenged or motivated. They know that simply staying on won't be good for either of you, and that perhaps your stint somewhere else might even pay dividends for them somewhere down the road.

Even if there are some hard feelings about your leaving, laying out your position clearly and politely is a wiser course of action than abruptly resigning from your job with no plausible explanation. And keeping in contact with the company won't hurt your chances of getting invited back, either.

During my time as a school business owner, one of my employees left abruptly for personal reasons, tendering her resignation over the phone.

Ordinarily, this wouldn't have been a huge problem. But when you're in charge of a classroom, and it's the middle of the school year, it's not easy to get a suitable replacement right away, especially for a Montessori-method institution that required specialized instructors.

So I came in to replace that teacher for half a year. On top of running the school and being enrolled in several courses, it was challenging both physically and emotionally, so I was quite unhappy with the situation.

Connie was a great employee and she was a tremendously valuable resource. I would have re-hired her without question under different circumstances. But she had left us in the lurch. So when she expressed interest in getting her old job back, we balked. After all, what if we had taken her back, only to have her leave us again without prior notice?

I don't mind people moving on to better things. And even though people are happy and may want to stay, they sometimes have to move with their partners to a different city, or leave for personal, health or professional, reasons.

I support people going further and higher in their careers. I try to practice an abundance mentality and I truly believe that what goes around comes around.

Like any employer, though, I do appreciate some advance notice when a resignation is tendered. And if that person goes out of their way to find an immediate replacement, then they're in my good books forever.

It's a good idea to keep in touch with as many of the people you've worked with in the past as possible.

Today's co-worker may very well be tomorrow's department head. And today's boss could even become your client tomorrow, if you decide to go into business for yourself. And in the age of internet-driven networking (e.g. Facebook, LinkedIn, and Twitter) it's become much easier to stay in touch with your previous and existing contacts.

At the very least, the people you've worked with throughout the years can serve as character or employment references. But remember: they'll only agree to vouch for you if you've shown proof of your dedication and ability to get things done.

CHAPTER 2

IS YOUR COMPANY STILL WORKING FOR YOU?

Getting people to buy into the company's mission, vision and values

Some company cultures are so heavily ingrained that they outlive their founders, and some promptly lose their way the minute the founder steps out of the picture. The minute the company owner or founder turns their back, the company's mission, vision and values are in the hands of the managers.

If the CEO and managers throughout the company aren't clear on and committed to these, then there's going to be a huge disconnect between what people say and what they actually do within the company. If there is no reinforcement, or if the company's values are muddled, everyone in the firm is going to work solely in their own self-interest.

That's when employees start to get demoralized and disillusioned. They conclude that the ideals are empty aspirations that aren't being lived up to by the people who are supposed to be upholding them. As a result, they may not develop any commitment to the company's mission, vision or values, and may also lose their passion for their work.

Ultimately, such employees and even managers may decide that the company is simply another opportunistic enterprise that doesn't care for them. This leads to a conclusion that's potentially lethal to any company: Employees come to believe the company doesn't really care; therefore they have to look out for themselves first.

And that's usually why employees end up hating their jobs inside it and also the reason that customers have such a lousy experience dealing with the company. Obviously, that's going to turn away customers in the short term. Over the longer term, that could seriously affect the company's standing and its very existence in the marketplace. Many once-mighty firms, like Circuit City or Linens n' Things, are now gone arguably as a result of such indifference from front line employees.

It's unfortunate, but as it grows in size, a company may lose its heart and soul along the way as a result of bringing in people who are driven purely by the pursuit of profit and failing to properly inculcate the company's values. **Unless the company's primary decision-makers and executive team genuinely buy into in the company's values and vision, it's going to be an uphill battle motivating people to set aside their own agenda and put customers first.**

Employees will be more inclined to act selflessly if they know that their boss will back them up, offer them recognition, and promote them. It's tough to do a really good job if your life at the office consists of trying to outwit your boss, work around their weaknesses, or help that person look good. Work is hard enough already that you really don't need the added burden of making up for other people's shortcomings just to keep your job.

Find out where you stand

One of the more unfortunate realities in the corporate landscape is that no matter how driven or dedicated you may be, if given a choice between keeping their own jobs or firing you, a number of managers wouldn't hesitate to hand you the pink slip. It's become rare these days for a supervisor or department head to put their own career on the line for a subordinate. The few that still do are highly prized both in company culture and by their team.

Knowing that someone is willing to go out on a limb for you encourages you to become loyal to that person. Loyalty is a two-way street, after all.

Let's face it though, in the real world, people at work are all busy looking out for themselves, and that includes your immediate bosses. They're not spending sleepless nights figuring out how to promote you or pay you better. They're preoccupied with looking good and figuring out how to climb the corporate ladder themselves. And they may or may not bring you up that ladder with them. It's unpleasant, but it's simply human nature. Unless helping you get ahead is part of their own performance metrics, they're not going to go out of their way to help to get you promoted.

You're going to have to be responsible for yourself. That's why it helps to adopt an entrepreneurial mindset and think like a free agent. The company purchases your labor; effectively it's your client. If this particular "client" isn't going to help you get ahead anytime soon, it's a good idea to look for a better client that's more employee focused.

Rather than wait for a bad situation to turn itself around, or wait for a difficult boss to retire so that you can fill their shoes, choose to be proactive with your career and make a special effort to stand out.

Make sure that your reputation as a person who gets things done spreads throughout the company. There are subtle ways to do this without having to go over your boss' head or making other people look bad. But you simply can't afford to let any one person block your efforts to get ahead.

Try to avoid getting in your boss' way and to allow him or her to get the credit for your work every now and then (but not every time). And keep an eye out to see if they reciprocate, or redirect the praise to you, where it belongs. If that never happens, then you'll know for sure that you're working for the wrong person. You're clearly wasting your time and will wait in vain for your efforts to be recognized.

If you see that they're indifferent to taking credit for the work of others, then be on your guard. A manager that is unwilling to spread around the glory may likely not hesitate to let others take the blame for their mistakes. When push comes to shove, you can safely bet that they're prepared to shove you out just to keep themselves in.

If you're stuck under such a person, quitting isn't the first resort, necessarily. Before you give your notice, consider whether to stay on or move to a different department with a more enlightened or a more caring boss.

If nothing presents itself, perhaps a new company altogether is where you need to go. There are caring companies out there that blend commercial success with a caring corporate culture. A good example is Deloitte, one of the biggest consulting firms in the world. They actually encourage their people to take sabbaticals, or take time off as needed for family.

The important thing is to learn your boss' true nature and intentions, to see whether they are open to helping you get ahead. If they are totally oblivious, or are focused completely on their own self interest, then you may assume that whatever you do likely isn't going to make any difference. If this is the case, it's probably best to update your resume and start having conversations with other companies within your industry.

If your boss won't point out your achievements to management or doesn't even recognize them, and if there's no better department to go to, or no position available outside your current unsatisfactory situation, you need to find a place where you're going to be appreciated. Your company may be a good place to be for some people, especially if it has a well articulated mission, vision and values, but it's clearly not working for you. More importantly it isn't really helping you advance your career. It's time to move on.

Don't let yourself fall into the trap of thinking "Well, maybe it'll get better," or "I'll just hang in there, someone will notice I'm working hard." Under an unappreciative manager you either have to go over their head, causing friction and poisoning the work relationship, or you have to get moving.

People and companies lose as a result of scarcity mentality

You may have witnessed some managers withholding information or training from their staff to prevent them from learning some new technology or process. They do this to ensure that they look more competent or knowledgeable than their subordinates. This may seem petty, but when their livelihood is on the line some higher-ups will fight tooth and nail to protect their turf, and they may resort to underhanded tactics if necessary.

Let's consider a situation where a company VP repeatedly states in meetings that there is a budget allocation for training to help everyone do their job better. When you ask your immediate boss if you can take advantage of this, you're told that there's no budget left for training this year in your department. So here you are getting two messages. Which one is the truth?

If the company is doing reasonably well, and you're seeing other people in other departments get training or being flown elsewhere for conferences while the people in your own department don't seem to be enjoying the same benefits, then you're probably being subjected to your supervisor's own personal agenda.

This may be a misguided effort to protect their own job by keeping you from knowing more than they do. In any case it's the "scarcity mentality" in action. **There really are people around who just don't believe that**

there are enough resources or opportunities in the world for everyone. This can be very frustrating.

Why should you have to put up with this, especially if you're being denied the benefit of training to help you do your job better and faster? This is one of those disconnects that prevents people from believing in the company, because one person in the organization is behaving as though their own career is the only thing that matters.

It's pretty sad but all too commonplace, unfortunately. And people in the executive offices often have no idea that this is happening. If your manager is acting like the stopper in the bottle, then higher management will never learn about the employees whose morale is slowly being drained as a result of that one self-serving person. Or if they do, they may refrain from making any comments, or taking action, especially if the department is fulfilling its minimal function or meeting its targets.

In the meantime, training resources are going to waste. People are leaving the company in frustration, while managers are fighting tooth and nail to preserve their influence and power. **Who ends up being the casualties of these petty office politics, though? The employees, and ultimately the firm itself.**

The passive and indifferent company

There are also companies that continuously hire and fire employees and whose fortunes rise and fall depending on how well or poorly the economy is doing. Such a company is one where the culture is sink or swim. There are usually employees who are immune from ever being fired while the ones who are not as bullet-proof are always in danger of losing their jobs.

This is a company that is in a reactive, rather than a proactive mode, and everyone is always in the dark about what's happening. The gossip machine is alive and well since people are only given information on a need-to-know basis, and stories get manufactured just to fill in the gaps.

There are favorites and pariahs, and you know who gets the perks and benefits without having to lift a finger and who will still get axed despite working long hours just to keep on proving their worth.

In some cases, this same company will even invest in the latest high tech equipment, fancy software, expensive office renovations, corporate events, or a slick web site while investing zero dollars to keep existing employees motivated or properly equipped to handle their jobs. Or they may keep people on contract permanently instead of hiring them as regular em-ployees to avoid giving them benefits.

Appearances, in some firms, have become more important than substance. If you make it to the inner circle, then you're safe. But if not, you could end up being one of the casualties in the initial round of layoffs.

If you happen to be employed by a company like this that is seemingly uncaring and lacks people sense, you'll need to watch out for yourself more carefully. **If you've become unhappy at work, your best bet is to take matters into your own hands and start looking for other opportunities that are better-suited to your abilities and your temperament.**

One person's poison really is another person's cup of tea. Some people thrive in highly competitive work environments. Many don't. If your company ends up being toxic to your health and sanity, you need to make your move. Instead of waiting to be let go one day, you should be the one to leave as soon as a good opportunity emerges. **Someone who regards the position you're about to leave as a dream job will come along to fill the void you've just left.** You and your soon-to-be ex-employer will both be much happier once you part ways.

You can learn how to confidently walk away from your job if it's no longer working for you and attract one that's a much better fit for you at **www.sittingprettycourse.com**

Sometimes, it's all personal

"Henry" worked for a software development company in Silicon Valley. He'd been enjoying a progressive and fruitful career at his firm for a few years.

Unfortunately, he didn't get off on the right foot with the VP of his department. Early in their working relationship, Henry had unintentionally put this VP on the spot. It was Henry's direct and forthright communication style that caused the incident. And although he regretted it, he felt that it had never been forgotten.

When layoffs were announced at the company during the recession of 2001, Henry was among one of those axed. He felt that other people who didn't work as hard as he did, or failed to produce tangible results, but who were in the VP's "inner circle" got to keep their jobs. While it's easy to dismiss Henry's observations as sour grapes, you do need to consider, especially if you're in a similar situation, how human relationships factor into these hiring and firing decisions.

There is a saying in business, and it also applies to the world of employment: **"People do business with people that they trust and that they like."**

Competence does matter, but if things boil down to letting one of two people go, then the one who is better liked often gets to stay. The same goes when a company is choosing to hire one of two people of nearly identical experience and competence. The one who has made an effort to establish prior contact and develop good rapport during the interview often wins.

If you have a difficult time getting along with the people in your department or your office, perhaps you should look for a firm or type of job that rewards rugged individualism (such as a sales position), or perhaps you should consider working for yourself. If you really love your job, you need to stay on reasonably good terms with your co-workers and particularly your immediate supervisors. Your job may depend on it.

Occasionally, the rug just gets pulled out from under you

Let's say that you've been working hard and getting along swimmingly with your boss, who decides to retire. All along this person has made sure that you get training, opportunity for advancement and credit for your work. But their successor turns out to not be as supportive.

Try as you might to build bridges with this person, there just isn't any chemistry; and this person seemingly isn't interested in looking out for anyone but themselves. That occasionally causes friction between the two of you. All of a sudden your budding career hits a dead end. **Your perfect company suddenly becomes a hell, all because of one simple change in personnel.**

Or let's say that things are all going smoothly and then an opportunity for the founder or owner to sell the company comes along. It may end up being a wonderful thing for that person, earning them a fortune as their just reward for their efforts. For everyone else in the company, though, it could be an entirely different story.

Mergers, especially, bring about a lot of tricky situations. Whole departments, such as accounting, human resources and the IT department are typically duplicated between merging companies. If the companies are at two separate locations most, or even all, employees may be retained. But if the two firms are in the same city or even country then some layoffs might be inevitable. Your career in this new larger company might even be in danger, especially if you're not one of the more highly specialized or skilled employees in the firm.

Company acquisitions don't just happen overnight. It typically takes 6 months to a year prior to getting the deal done, and another 6 months to a year for everything to get settled into place after it's signed. A year from your first notification about the impending acquisition is enough time for you to evaluate your options, inside and outside the company.

If you haven't networked a lot before, it's time to start practicing and update your resume. If nothing bad happens, then you've lost nothing by preparing for the worst. If the rug gets pulled out from under you, then you're already prepared for this worst-case scenario, and hopefully have some alternative options that you can take advantage of immediately.

To learn how to network effectively and be able to organize more information gathering meetings from potential employers, refer to **www.sittingprettycourse.com**

CHAPTER 3
THE IMPORTANCE OF RELATION-SHIPS

Performance is only half the battle

Although a company is like a tiny little universe that consists of employees above, around and below you, one of the key factors that can make or break your career is whether or not you've got your immediate boss on your side. This person is your main "client", and the single most important person that you have to please. **If you really don't get along with your supervisor, then it doesn't really matter how hard you work.** You probably won't be getting that promotion.

On the other hand, people who are able to build good relationships with their bosses and other important decision makers tend to move very far up the corporate food chain. It seems unfair but there you go. Doing a good job—a great job even—is usually only half the battle.

Decision-makers also understand that with higher responsibility comes the all-important function of having to manage people. They often promote people based on their ability to get along with everybody else and enlist their cooperation. Technically gifted employees are valuable, but if they have poor interpersonal skills, then they'll be passed over for promotion by people who may not be as good with the nuts and bolts of the job, but have the ability to organize and lead others.

Simply going to work and doing what you're good at isn't enough to help you to get ahead these days. **You have to develop a reputation, not only for doing a great job, but also for being great to work with**.

The key then is balance. You need to be good at the work you do, but not to the exclusion of your co-workers. Be careful that you're not creating a little silo that's off limits to other human beings. For one thing, no one's going to promote you, or even care if you lose your job, if they don't know you exist.

Companies can also be highly interactive environments where people have to get together and disband as teams as they work on various projects, and where everyone acts interchangeably as "clients" and "suppliers". Co-workers will sometimes act as your clients whenever they need things from you, putting you in the position of supplier. Roles will switch every now and then, but generally, companies are never good places to be a lone wolf.

That's why it's important to enlist the support of people around you. You may be totally focused on your work, which is good. Just don't completely ignore the people around you. The workplace does still consist of human beings, who thrive on a certain level of interaction. While it's not necessary to develop deep friendships in an office the way you would in school, you can certainly make yourself pleasant to be around and easy to work with.

Make your boss your number one ally

Although it's important to turn in a great performance, you also need to be in the good graces of the person who holds the key to your future, and that's your immediate boss. You need to not only make this person care, but to also make it in their best interest to promote you. Otherwise, it will be more difficult for you to get ahead.

Some people try to undermine their boss, especially if they think that the person just one step above them seems like a nice person (mistaking niceness for weakness) or is less technically skilled than they are. But those people still have power, and they have the support and backing of even more powerful decision-makers within the firm.

"Ray" worked for a few years at a technology company where his immediate boss was a bit younger and technically inexperienced. Ray felt that his boss was not as supportive or competent, and failed to display any empathy. So he took a willful stance and would periodically engage in arguments with his boss and turn down assignments whenever possible. Ray is now gone, a victim of one of the firm's round of layoffs. His former boss' career, though, continues to thrive.

If you think you can go over your boss' head, think again. Most owners and influential people in the firm stand behind your managers and supervisors, and they want to know that your manager sees you as an asset before they'll go to bat for you or hand you added responsibility. It's far better to seek the support of your boss, rather than try to get this person out of the way. **Working against your immediate boss is a very dangerous game to play, and one which you're likely to lose.**

If you think you're a rising superstar who doesn't always get the proper recognition, consider these:

- *Are you really performing well?*

- *Is your boss aware of and sympathetic to your career goals?*

- *Do you make a point of maintaining good relations with people around you?*

If the answer to any of these questions is "No" then you need to fix the situation. A few hours of overtime, a short chat outlining your aspirations to your boss, or even a quiet drink after work with your co-workers may do a great deal to bring you closer to your goals.

If you've answered "Yes" to the three previous questions, consider:

- *Is the company culture a good fit for you?*

- *Is your boss actively working with you, and not against, you? (See Chapter 2)*

- *Does the opportunity you're after exist within the company?*

If you answer any of these questions "No," it's almost certainly time to do some research and talk to other people at other companies to see what else is out there. There are tons of other places to work, and perhaps better people to work for.

Again, you have to be responsible for your own career. If you really think your boss is a complete idiot or an uncaring person, you can try and adjust your attitude, ask to be transferred, or move on. **There's no point to working for someone you don't respect; and**

no use in working in a place where you're not respected either.

If you've decided to stick to your job, you have to get into the radar screens of decision makers. You won't get very far by working in total anonymity. Shyness and humility are two things that are not going to help you get promoted. If you want to get noticed in a corporate environment, a bit of daring and assertiveness helps.

So appeal to the bottom line: ask for more responsibility. And don't be afraid to approach these decision makers and strike up an intelligent conversation with them every now and then to remind them of your existence. Find out their personal interests and see if you can't get involved in what they're doing, too. You can probably find common ground without having to fake interest.

Getting ahead at work is like selling yourself. You have to get noticed, encourage the decision-makers to talk to other people about the quality of your work, win their trust and loyalty, and finally get them to sign off on your promotion. That doesn't happen by accident.

As with sales, it takes deliberate planning and special effort to develop a relationship until such time that the prospect is ready to pick you over your competitors.

Customers get good service if employees are treated well

For employees to connect with what the company is about, it takes more than town hall meetings and corporate retreats for them to get sold on the company's mission, vision and values. That's all just words on paper.

What brings them to life is committed action, all the way from the top, to apply this mission, vision and values to everyday interactions between employees and customers. **Only by consistently being on purpose, on target and value centered will companies win the hearts and minds of people who work within the company and do business with it.**

Customers will be treated the same way that management treats its employees. You are the face of your company. So if you come across a crabby employee at another firm, that's a barometer of how that company is run. On the other hand, if you come across a very caring customer service rep, the corporate culture has a lot to do with that.

It's people who bring life to abstract concepts like mission and values statements. If you want to get great results from people around you, they have to know first that you'll stick out your neck for them. If all you care about is your own career, then they won't show any regard for anyone else but themselves as well. If you want your own boss, or your subordinates, to go to bat for you, you need to show a bit of your own loyalty to these people first.

There's no reason you can't help other people as you nurture your own career. **It is possible to care for others as you look out for yourself.** It's good business and it's certainly good for morale. People are just as sensitive to caring managers as they are to uncaring managers. Apathy at the highest levels just causes people to shut down and become completely self-centered, or otherwise seek kinder and more caring places to work.

You can demonstrate leadership by helping out the new hires in the company. Think of it as an opportunity to train your replacement as you move higher up the ladder, or for when you leave the company. It'll never hurt your reputation to leave the company in better shape than you found it.

The importance of getting feedback and valuable advice

Companies that have a strong expertise and reputation in a particular area will attract the best candidates. But for these people to stay, they need to know that their workplace also has a human heart. **A company has to be people-centered as well as profit-centered.** The minute people feel that they're being undervalued or unappreciated, mediocrity sets in. Consequently, employees will be prompted to just work for their paychecks and treat the company's customers with less enthusiasm and compassion than they deserve.

Implementing a strong and consistent feedback system helps people to know exactly where they stand, and allows them to pinpoint areas for improvement. Getting input from managers, co-workers and customers lets people know how to do their jobs better. And letting all this information flow freely allows people to trust each other more and work together more smoothly.

Seek ideas and ask for suggestions from people around you. Don't be afraid to say "Hey Pat, I really liked what you did with that project. Would you mind giving me some ideas to help me deliver a good presentation?" Never be afraid to ask your manager: "Ted, do you have any suggestions about how I can improve my performance (or get on the fast track for promotion)?" When people can see that their input is being sought out and taken seriously, they learn to reciprocate and become committed to each other's advancement and success.

Another way to improve your chances of moving up in your current company is by finding a mentor. There are formal and informal types of mentoring. Formal mentorship programs usually pair up an employee with a senior worker or manager. This helps you benefit from the valuable wisdom and experience of a veteran employee.

A mentor system also creates more opportunities for dialogue and communication. If your company has such a program, ask if you can participate. Or simply go directly to the person that you want as a mentor to see if they might be able to spend an hour or two a week to share some of their wisdom and experience with you.

You may also use mentoring on your own time. Find someone in your job, or the career or position you think you want. Ask if they'll let you job-shadow them for a day or two, or whether you can just spend an hour a week with them to learn more.

Loyalty must be earned

Loyalty and trust don't come automatically. They have to be earned over time. That applies upwards as well as downward. Have you ever taken somebody else's sales territory, or inherited someone's else's staff? Did they greet you with open arms, or were they being cautious and trying to feel you out? Most likely it's the latter. People have established orders and hierarchies at work, and you violate these at your peril.

That's why you have to be extremely careful when you step into someone's shoes. It's very easy to hurt people's feelings and to insult someone's memory inadvertently, especially if they were particularly revered as a leader or partner.

I worked briefly as a sales representative for a big pharmaceutical company early in my career. I had to go visit doctors and nurses in hospitals. No one explained to me that there were tightly guarded power-structures within these places. I promptly shot myself in the foot by trying to bypass the gatekeepers in these structures instead of attempting to work with them. My manager passed on some strong complaints about me from customers regarding my lack of understanding about the system or showing enough respect for certain people within the hierarchy.

I stayed only for about 6 months. I was unhappy every day that I went to work and was relieved when I decided to leave my job. To their credit, the company encouraged me to try other avenues and even gave me an option to work in a different sales territory, just to get my feet wet.

The company's show of support was encouraging, but it wasn't enough to keep me in a job that I'd realized simply wasn't a good fit for me. Fortunately I was smart enough to admit it early on, rather than to stay on and try to make it work. I could have lost many years of my life clinging on to something that I didn't really have any excitement or passion for.

The company I worked for also learned that new people couldn't just be thrown at the deep end right from the start. And despite their loyalty to the company itself, existing customers were not always helpful or friendly to new sales reps. The new hires still had to win the loyalty of these long-time customers, who had developed a strong bond with the former sales rep that didn't automatically transfer to that person's replacement. That's also how I learned an important lesson: **You have to keep winning people's trust and confidence every single day in order keep them loyal to you.**

In "The 7 Habits of Highly Effective People" Dr. Stephen Covey talks about continuously making deposits into an "emotional bank account", which is another way of describing how we have to constantly invest time and energy to the people in our personal and professional networks, so that they will in turn continue to look out for us. (Learn the right—and the wrong—ways to network at **www.sittingprettycourse.com**)

So while you may be thinking about, or working on, a change of department, job, or even industry, **you need to maintain the best possible relationships with your boss and co-workers** all the time, every single day. This helps pave your way out of an unsatisfactory position to something better. More importantly, this will help them to retain fond memories of you, which is how you want to be remembered, especially if they are contacted by your future employers who are doing a background check on you.

CHAPTER 4
PERFORMANCE IS A MUST

Business downturns are sometimes used to cull non-performers

If you're not delivering, the company most likely won't hold on to you, especially if your performance is sub par or your negative attitude doesn't change. **More than a few companies readily take advantage of business downturns to lay off people who aren't suitable.**

Companies that have mass layoffs tend to not re-hire certain people once the economy gets better. What they've done is use an economic situation to clear the decks of non-performing assets; mainly people who don't contribute to the bottom line, people who are difficult to get along with or people they prefer not to keep on for any reason.

It's pretty easy to tell who the top performers are. **It's much better to work hard so that you can develop a reputation as one of the stars.** Good news travels quickly, and bad news travels even faster. This is a big reason why you can't fake performance at the office. People around you will know it when you're coasting. And it will definitely come back to haunt you in the end.

You don't want to turn off potential employers with half-hearted effort. These days it isn't very hard to find out this kind of information. People do talk. And now there's Facebook and other social media sites to spread the news even faster.

That's another reason that you should do a stellar job in all you do, wherever you go: **You always want to be invited back.** There's nothing more gratifying and cost-effective for a company than to have you trained and educated at somebody else's expense. Many firms wouldn't mind if you went away for a bit if they can get you back with added knowledge and skills.

To turn in a good performance every day, you need to think like a contractor. There is no coasting along when you're a contractor. You're too easy to replace. And there usually aren't any hard feelings when you are let go, since deliverables are clearly stated and mutually agreed upon at the very start.

Contractors who fail to deliver on their contracts usually don't last long, or don't get their contracts renewed.

Contracting is on the rise

In his groundbreaking book "In Search Of Excellence" Tom Peters first talks about more and more people becoming contractors rather than salaried employees. This arrangement has a lot of obvious advantages. Despite the lack of stability, in terms of job tenure, people tend to charge more per hour and consequently end up earning greater income than their employee counterparts.

As self-employed professionals, they typically end up paying less tax on the money they earn as a result of being able to write off various business expenses (see your accountant to learn the benefits of incorporating). On the employer side companies end up saving on benefits, vacation and severance pay, which can be a heavier expense burden than the price difference in the hourly rate between a contractor and an employee.

There are advantages for contractors too: Having built good relationships with the stakeholders, they're sometimes more plugged into what's happening in the company. They usually get a heads-up when something important happens before everyone else does. Contractors don't usually get the rug pulled out from under them without prior notice.

They work on a series of contracts with various employers that they prefer to work with, and are able to please more easily. Consequently, they are able to solidify their careers by being able to work with clients that are a good fit and who come back repeatedly for the same brand of service provided by the contractor.

They also know that their most valuable currency is their reputation in the business. **Contractors' services are in demand once their reputation gets established**, and they have their pick of jobs that are constantly thrown their way. As a result, they have much greater career stability over the long term.

Sounds pretty great, doesn't it? If you learn to think like a contractor, you can enjoy the same advantages.

Eight things you need to learn from contractors:

1. Contractors don't think in terms of "forever"

Contractors have a different attitude with regards to their employers. They know that at any time their services can be terminated by either party if one of them feels unhappy about the arrangement. There is no long-term obligation to stay. Consequently, contractors tend to approach work a bit differently, knowing that they have to prove themselves each and every day to their clients, since their employability depends on their ability to deliver consistently.

2. Contractors never pretend to be busy

As a contractor, your services are no longer required once the project is complete or work has finished (or in some unfortunate cases ground to a halt). You may be called back once a new project kicks in but the employer doesn't have to pay you the whole year round whether there is work to be done or not. Consequently, there are no lull periods or times when a contractor has to pretend that they are busy so that their employer will keep them on the payroll. So in thinking like a contractor, you need to learn to keep yourself busy. If work is slow, look for something useful to do. If you don't see something, ask. Your manager will appreciate your initiative.

3. Contractors are never invisible, nor regarded as a threat

In the world of free-agenting, you are never buried under layers of staff where no one sees what you're doing and no one knows who you are. You're constantly measured on your performance and the results that you generate. Regular employees know immediately that you are an "outsider" and hardly ever look at you as a threat. To them, you are simply a vendor or a supplier.

While this allows the contractor a greater level of neutrality, they're still obliged to develop good working relationships with the people they work with. Although other contractors can be hired in your stead, a great relationship is tough to replace.

4. Contractors understand the value of collaboration

If you've been in a corporate environment long enough, you'll understand that there is greater reward and recognition for team players than for the "lone wolf." Contractors still have to win over the people they work alongside of to get their cooperation and support, especially if they're introducing something new or different to the company. They also have to deliver and show progress on a daily basis, in order for their contracts to be renewed by the decision-makers.

5. Contractors know that good (and bad) things don't last

Contractors understand that companies that do well most of the time are sometimes subject to economic downturns and poor sales and, as a result, may terminate contracts from time to time. Therefore, they don't expect lifetime employment from one company. They know that each working relationship has a definite start and end, and are constantly on the lookout for other clients to serve.

They move on very easily and are able to adapt to new corporate environments quickly. Even if the current client decides to re-hire them contractors may not necessarily sign on again, because they've already committed to working with a different client on another project, or simply because they don't want to. Thinking like a contractor can give you almost the same degree of freedom.

6. Contractors live and die by their knowledge and expertise

Contractors have a greater motivation to bring value to the table. They are painfully aware that their continued employability depends on good word of mouth, which in turn is dependent on their ability to consistently do a great job each and every time for every employer. As a result, they also work hard at constantly expanding their knowledge base and deepening their level of experience to stay on top of their game and be continuously regarded as a valuable resource.

7. Contractors don't always say "Yes" to every job offer

Not all clients who clamor for a contractor's services end up being a good fit. Rather than say yes to everyone that is interested to hire them, they tend to be choosier about whom they would work with, and they don't take a termination personally. They know that the right client will see the value of their work and agree to pay them what they are worth, and also give them good word of mouth advertising once the project is done. They also know that going into business with potentially difficult clients is a losing situation that they should avoid at all costs, as both parties will only end up being unhappy.

8.   Contractors have an abundance mentality

Contractors don't wait for a bad situation to turn around by itself. When a particular client or job turns out to be more trouble than its worth, they simply accept the fact that this is not the right situation for them and terminate the contract themselves. They know that there are a ton of clients out there, many of whom will be a better fit. They have an abundance mentality that enables them to thrive and to keep things in perspective. **They focus their efforts to attract not just any type of client, but the right type of client.**

Once you adopt the contractor mentality, you'll be able to better match your ability and your experience to the right company and also get a better compensation package.

Know your own value and what the competition is charging

The contractor knows what his or her work is worth. As an employee, if you're performing well, and if you know the value you bring to the table, and how valuable that makes you to other potential employers, then you shouldn't feel awkward asking for a raise.

Being fully aware of what the going rate is for other people doing the same job, you can ask for comparable pay and perks with complete confidence, knowing that you can get it somewhere else. If you deliver genuine value, the marketplace is going to pay you what you're really worth.

If your employers know that they could lose you to a higher bidder, they'll try to do whatever is necessary to keep you happy. Of course if you're just doing the minimum there's no incentive for them to pay you more than just enough to keep you from leaving.

Know who else is on the playing field

Contractors know the competition, what they're charging, and the client base for their shared field of work. Knowing the other players in your industry helps your career. Knowing what the going rate is for your position is valuable information that you can use to your benefit. Knowing decision-makers at other firms is another ace to have up your sleeve. All this information strengthens your bargaining position.

If you know your services are in great demand, you can negotiate from a position of strength when you ask for a raise or a promotion. You can walk away from a job if you feel that you're not getting a fair shake since you know that there are others out there you can easily work for. You don't need to resort to bluffing, or worse, to playing a bad hand if your boss calls your bluff.

Know how to work smarter, not longer

You can certainly spend fifty to a hundred hours at the office working as hard as you can. However, if you can spend just an extra hour or two a week gathering intelligence and building relationships throughout your industry, then you'll be in a much stronger position than if you simply worked longer. You may very well end up exploring various opportunities in a series of companies, broadening and deepening your knowledge and expertise as you go.

Know where the opportunities are and who to call

Thinking like a contractor means thinking as though you're running your own business. A business typically doesn't rely on one client. That would be dangerous, especially if your sole client decides to stop buying your services (i.e. fires you). You need to have other clients who know the quality of your work and are willing to pay for—and hire—your services the second they learn that you become available.

Since most employees can only realistically work for one employer at a time, what they can do is establish relationships with various people at different companies within their industry. That way, they have a pool of alternatives to pick and choose from if ever they are laid off, or if they choose to move elsewhere on their own accord.

Know when to move on

When the job's done, or the contract has ended, the contractor moves on. In employee terms, there might come a day that you and your employer have to part ways. If the owner or company president decides that it needs to trim staff, you may end up being one of the unlucky ones picked for this latest round of layoffs. It might be beyond the control of your supervisor to pick who has to go. They may simply be the bearer of bad news, despite a personal wish to keep you on board.

You don't have to feel stigmatized if you've just been let go, regardless of the reason: whether you didn't get along with your boss, or the job just wasn't the right fit. If you've conditioned yourself to keep searching for the right company, there's no need for any hard feelings if your current employment situation doesn't work out. Just take your severance pay (if you're entitled) and move on to another employer. "It just wasn't the right fit," has become quite acceptable to companies these days.

Many companies can now fire employees without just cause, and some even insert this specific provision into employment contracts. You may be outraged, and be thinking about litigation to get your job back. But consider carefully. Even if you did sue your firm and win, do you really want to work in a place that disliked you enough to fire you for no specific reason?

If you're no longer wanted at a firm, just shrug your shoulders and move on. Why try and force your way back in? That's like trying to keep a toxic relationship going because you're so used to being with this other person, even though it's not really good for either of you.

Wouldn't you rather work for a firm that appreciates what you do and also supports and promotes you? **If you've learned to develop an abundance mentality, you'll always remember that there really are tons of fish in the sea**.

Think win-win if you decide to leave (or stay)

Maintaining a contractor mentality as an employee also means you should be constantly on the lookout for other potential clients who may be able to use your services. You may have to get work elsewhere one day, especially if your current employer has to let go of employees due to a business downturn, or is forced to close their business.

Keep in mind that your slot can be always filled by someone hungrier for your job. You, on the other hand, will end up helping another company who may desperately need your services and doesn't mind paying what you're asking. It's a win-win situation for both you and your current employer.

There's nothing wrong with always looking for the best deal and work arrangement for yourself. Your company is also constantly looking for ways to reduce costs, which may involve trimming staff or outsourcing. You'll be doing your current employer a great disservice if you're unhappy with responsibilities that you have, or frustrated with not getting ahead, or not getting the salary that you feel you deserve.

In the end, the company's clients are going to be the victims of all this negative feeling. So you might as well research a few places where you'll feel more motivated to carry out the company's mission and vision, preferably before you're let go or forced to look for work elsewhere for some reason. You'll be happier if you have an idea exactly where you're going to land, what the terrain is like and whether the natives are friendly.

Always be looking

When you're out doing information gathering meetings with various potential employers (or "clients") the best type of research is a two-sided, win-win meeting with each prospect where the outcome is uncertain.

These meetings are relaxed, honest and extremely helpful in determining whether this is the right place for you to work on one hand, and whether you're the right hire for them on the other. They know you're working and not desperate, so your level of desirability increases.

You'll probably need to check out a few possibilities to get a sense of what's available, rather than accepting the first job offer that comes your way. Why not use one or two lunch breaks a week to see what's out there? And if you get into the habit of constantly evaluating other opportunities and companies that are out there, you enhance the prospect of finding one where you'll be happy to come to work every day.

If you're only going to an interview once every 3 to 5 years, you're not as likely to find your ideal situation. You'll also be too focused on winning the job that you're interviewing for even if it's not the right one for you. You'll lose some pretty valuable time that you're never going to get back if you grab the first offer and it ends up not being the right fit, forcing you to leave at some point in the future. **Instead, try and learn how well each company that you're interviewing for is suited to your talents, experience and values.**

It's all a numbers game

So try to get lots of face-to-face information gathering meetings. Having many good jobs to choose from is a good problem that you should have. Competing with 99 other people for a single job, when times are hard and competition is intense, is no fun at all.

If all of this sounds like long, hard exercise, or something that's totally beyond your comfort zone then, well, it could be. But you need to step out of that comfort zone. The old "let's-open-the-classifieds-section-to-see-what's-out-there-today" approach is akin to picking the lowest hanging fruit. It's so easy that everyone else will be doing it, and it's far harder to fight off 99 other candidates than it is to cultivate one opportunity all by yourself.

The sweetest fruit is higher up, and requires a bit of extra effort. The information gathering meeting requires courage and imagination. And it isn't for everyone. But if you were like everyone, you probably wouldn't have picked up this book. **You're here because you're sincerely ready for change and are willing to take your work—and your life—to the next level.**

Learn how to properly set up information gathering meetings and discover other job-winning alternatives to mass-mailing resumes at **www.sittingprettycourse.com**

CHAPTER 5
CREATE YOUR OWN CAREER INSUR-ANCE POLICY

Look out the window once in a while

Contractors don't ever imagine they'll always be working for the same client, and neither should you. **Things might be going well now, but that doesn't mean that they always will.**

Don't forget to look out for yourself while you look out for your current employer. It's not inconceivable for your company to let you go due to stiff competition, or business losses. So keep your eyes peeled for the writing on the wall, and be ready to contact members of your network to help you get back on your feet.

Changes in ownership, new bosses or alterations in the corporate culture always bring upheaval and what may seem fine today may not be tomorrow. That's why it pays to keep looking at what's happening outside your company. You don't want to be caught off-guard working for an industry that's on its way out.

Consider the oil business, for example. Now that consumers are clamoring for the automotive sector to develop cleaner energy sources like hydrogen or electricity the days of oil as a motor fuel are likely numbered. Companies that belong to this industry, and the companies that rely on the oil extraction business, are most likely going to shrink.

Or if you're working in the tobacco business, be mindful that smokers are less accepted socially than at any time since World War I, and more and more restaurants and bars have imposed a no-smoking policy. Advertising is restricted, and marketing to youth is illegal. That significantly impacts the industry, and your job.

Be sensitive to what's happening

In the wake of the sub-prime mortgage debacle of 2008 the investment banking, securities trading, and brokerage industries were hit hard. There are now fewer jobs in this sector because huge institutions, like Lehman Brothers, Bear Stearns or Merrill Lynch, have either disappeared or were absorbed by other firms.

Goldman Sachs and Morgan Stanley are now subject to tighter regulations. Most of the giant-killing upheaval happened within a single 3-month period.

In 2009 more than 100 newspaper businesses closed, and over 10,000 jobs have been lost in this industry alone. Whether you blame the internet for changing reading habits of consumers (to web-based news articles), or for the loss of advertising (to Craigslist for example), this shift is a tremendous one, especially since newspapers have been around for centuries.

Even the book publishing business has been severely affected, primarily by Amazon, and pretty soon by eBook readers. If you're a writer or a journalist or otherwise connected to the printing or publishing industry, this has huge implications.

Things can change very quickly, and the last thing you need is to have blinders over your eyes, especially if you put them on yourself.

We're all essentially problem solvers

Avoid being defined by your company or industry. Like accountants or lawyers, make sure that you realize that your skills are portable and can be used in a totally different industry or in a different city, with only minor tweaking or upgrading.

All work is essentially problem-solving. And good problem solvers should have no shortage of work anywhere. Companies exist to solve the world's various problems and make money doing it. Construction firms exist to solve the problem of creating personal living spaces and work places. Hospitals solve the problem of illness. Legal firms exist to solve problems that arise between people, or between people and companies or the state. Your problem solving ability is your biggest transportable asset. It can easily be applied to an entirely different industry and, with a bit of re-training, even a whole new career.

Law enforcement personnel, for example, can check out opportunities in private security companies or even personal security work, where the client hires their protection directly. Or if you're working as a letter carrier, you could look into what's happening in the corporate courier industry. Stockbrokers have expertise they can use for any sales-related position. If you can solve a problem in one industry, there's no reason you can't continue to do the same thing in another.

Taking your leave gracefully

If you've lost your passion or your will to get out of bed, then you owe it to your employer to either find new motivation or leave for greener pastures. Why not try to help find your replacement and clear out so that they can come in?

If your view of the company is exceedingly negative and you can't find anything good in the situation, then it's definitely time to move on. You deserve to get a job that's right for you, and the company that you're working for deserves to have someone that really wants your position.

People switch jobs several times throughout their career

In one survey, it was discovered that people changed jobs an average of 10 times between the ages of 18 and 36. Since people don't stop working at 36, they probably move at least once or twice more after that age, bringing the job-switching average to at least 12 times.

What's keeping you tied down to one company?

On average, as many as one out of every two employees have recently thought about changing or quitting their jobs. A recent survey suggested that 70 percent of Americans dread coming to work every day. Consider these questions:

- Why is the comfort of routine more powerful than the impetus to move to a better place, where working conditions and pay are superior?

- Why do we not manage our careers better?

- What's so difficult about change that we resist it, even if it is for our own good?

Seventy percent—It's a staggering number: Nearly three-quarters of the working population doesn't want to go to work at their current jobs. Considering that half of our waking hours are spent at work or getting to the office or factory, that's a stunning amount of misery that people carry on a daily basis.

It's also a significant amount of stress on the human body. Although poor nutrition and lack of sleep and exercise hasten illness and disease, it's often what happens in our heads that has the greatest impact. More people than ever before are showing up at hospitals and clinics for ailments that start with the mind and manifest themselves by aggravating existing illness or weakening the immune system, allowing new ones in.

Stress can kill, and it could be killing you, even if you're so used to stifling your frustrations at work that you don't realize you're unhappy. Although you may not recognize a bad situation, your body certainly does.

Have you ever thought about what else is out there for you?

Wouldn't you prefer to whistle a happy tune every day, and get paid for the privilege? Have you talked to people doing the same jobs as you in other companies?

If not, what's stopping you? **Are you waiting for things to "sort themselves out"?**

It's amazing what human beings can subject themselves to, even when they can easily dig themselves out of a hole they've been stuck in. While it may take some work and risk to climb out, usually we end up better off.

Looking for work, socializing with other people in our industry or staying connected with the people throughout our personal and work history can be a pain in the neck. You've got enough to do in a day, right?

Most people would rather do it once the need arises rather than do the necessary upkeep work, **just as how, with our health, we tend to do something only when something goes wrong.** What could be easy ends up being infinitely more difficult, expensive, and inconvenient in the end. We're used to being more reactive than proactive.

So how can you look after yourself better? If you're one of those unhappy workers, the time to act is now. Here are a few strategies to get started with:

- **Take courses to perform your job better**. You may discover a new love for the old job when you gain fresh insights.

- **Use after-work time to research other more interesting jobs and industries**. That way you can keep on earning a steady income during the day, and slowly transition into your desired line of work.

- **Take a course in an entirely new area of interest**. You can also use your free time to simply test the waters and see if you really like this new field that you've been dreaming of pursuing.

- **Update your resume every 6 months at least**. Once your name starts to spread, having your resume handy will enable you to pass these around quickly when they are requested. This will also help to remind you about your successes at work before they fade from memory.

There are many lawyers, for instance, who no longer want to practice law. Or accountants who want to do something totally different. Or engineers who really want to be musicians, but were told at an early age that that wasn't a "practical" line of work. Many of us yearn to live a different life, but remain too fearful or too comfortable to leave, especially if the work they no longer love has afforded them a certain lifestyle.

Realizing that we're unhappy is one thing. But doing something about it is something else entirely. Here are two reasons people stubbornly hold on to a job they no longer enjoy:

1. Discomfort with the prospect of starting over

Most people don't want start from scratch and re-establish themselves in an entirely new company or a new location, understandably. Taking a huge cut in pay can hurt, especially if lifestyle really matters to you.

Change is often uncomfortable, even though it can lead to greater happiness down the road.

2. Fear of being perceived as having no focus or direction

Many people are concerned about what people will say or think: "You switched from chartered accountancy to owning and managing a bed-and-breakfast? Are you nuts?" It's common to fear that hiring managers may be put off by an excessive number of positions on your resume. But switching jobs these days is no longer the taboo that it used to be.

Statistically, Americans will change careers at least three times over the course of their working lives. In other countries the number is as high as eight.

However, more people are becoming less averse to major career changes and fewer people are surprised at them for doing it. **People want to be happy with what they're doing, on top of just taking home a regular paycheck.**

Part of this is generational: people born just before or during the Depression were simply happy to have work. They and the post-war "Baby-Boom" generation saw themselves doing the same type of work for pretty much the rest of their lives. But the Boomers, as they aged, and their children in the X and Y generations are looking for validation and fulfillment through their work, and workers of all ages have learned to separate their jobs from their personal lives.

Stay happy, stay connected

Most employees, given a choice between happiness and a big paycheck, pick happiness. **But there's no reason to trade off happiness for compensation. You can have both.** And you deserve to.

That's why it makes sense to be on the lookout for other opportunities even, or maybe especially, when everything is going fine.

You can always make money, but you can never get back time and you can afford to waste very little of it. If you start to feel that you're not getting paid enough, you can certainly ask for a raise. But do a bit of research first to determine whether your situation really is unfair or not. You have to put things into perspective, and not expect too much sometimes, because different companies have different levels of resources.

A 10,000-person firm will most likely be able to pay better than one that employs just three people, especially if it's been around for a hundred years compared to the smaller one that's just been around for five. Your research should help you discover whether your salary is all your company can afford.

Few people are ever happy making the same salary ten years after joining the company. Families grow, goods and service costs increase over time. What you're making now won't be enough to pay for your needs tomorrow.

If your current salary makes you unhappy, and there's not much more that your present employer can offer you in pay, benefits, or responsibility, then having done your research beforehand can help you decide whether to pull out now or hang on awhile. **Remember, no one wants an unhappy employee.**

Keep looking for the best fit for your skill set and level of experience. Have serious conversations with other interested parties. At the very least, you'll find out what you're worth, and what the market is willing to pay. Not all people will move purely out of salary considerations, of course. Having a nice office, a close-to-home location, good co-workers and a supportive boss are definitely considerations that are on top of other people's lists.

It also pays to make contacts and strengthen friendships with people in other firms. Companies are constantly on the lookout for talent. And if you're not on their radar screen, then you won't be contacted by these companies once an opening becomes available.

People also resign and move on to other companies (if you're following this advice you could soon be one of them), so despite what you're hearing about high levels of unemployment, there are vacancies that occur all the time. You just need to be at the right place at the right time to take advantage of them once these come up.

Here's one place to find a position: **Look for a company that's just had a round of layoffs.** Not everyone who survives the layoffs wants to stay. For one thing, there's more work for not much more salary. People may walk away from their jobs if a particular manager or co-worker has left, and sometimes a really good manager may take people along to a new company.

Another possibility with such companies is that they'll discover that they've cut too deep and will embark on a new round of hiring to replenish their ranks. You can be one of the new hires.

Never be in a reactive position

Look for work before you need it. **Be looking out for all kinds of opportunities at all times.** If you only take 15 to 30 minutes every day to evaluate the opportunities that are out there, then you'll never have to worry about being out of work for long periods, or depleting your savings as you look for a new job.

Building a network of contacts at other places where you can work is the best insurance for your career. You can find out how to develop your networking "muscle" and create better results in your job search at **www.sittingprettycourse.com**

CHAPTER 6
MANAGING YOUR CAREER IN THE 21ST CENTURY

Be mindful of your sanity first and foremost, and the rest will follow

If you've done a personal assessment (use the PERSONAL AND CAREER Planner at www.personalandcareerplanner.com) and figured out what makes you tick, you might learn that either:

- You're exactly where you need to be; or

- You still need to find that ideal place to work, or that thing that will motivate you to jump out of bed and shout "Thank God it's Monday!"

If you haven't sat down to really think about what motivates you, then you're simply flying by the seat of your pants, and it's more likely a hit and miss situation, where it could be more miss.

Consider the 70% to 30% ratio of unhappy-to-happy people that was mentioned in the last chapter. That's a grim statistic, and it's a great likelihood that you may be part of the 70%.

If you're unhappy with what you're doing, pay may not really matter much at this point. You will definitely need your salary to support yourself and perhaps a family. But how much longer can you stand working for a company you despise at a job you detest?

Want to know the worst of this dire situation? It's being completely dependent on your income and hating what you do. Not every highly paid hedge-fund manager, I.T. consultant, or lawyer, for example, wants to keep on doing what they're doing. Sometimes, it's just so risky, stressful, or uninteresting that people just want to quit there and then. But they can't.

Well as the old saying goes, "Money can't buy happiness … but it sure buys a better class of misery." So people can be still be miserable despite owning a mansion, luxury automobile, or other symbols of wealth. It may be a miserable life, but at least it's a comfortable one, and comfort's what we're all after, right?

Figure out what you really want

It turns out that it ain't necessarily so. **Many people would take a pay cut if it meant doing what they really love to do**.

A huge number of people are still looking for their "what," or their purpose; that magic thing that captures their imagination and engages their creative spark. And they realize deep down inside that time isn't on their side. Yet many of them continue to drag themselves to work to make some money (or even lots of it) doing a job that isn't making them happy, while time and opportunities continue to pass them by.

A lot of people aren't willing to take a hard look in the mirror, truly. They don't bother to sit down and figure themselves out, and also forget to hope and to dream. And they believe themselves, perhaps, to be happy at that moment.

People build up an image of themselves and often dislike to examine it too closely. Introspection can be quite painful. But it can also lead us back to the right path. There's nothing that should stop you from changing course completely if you need to. **Change can happen in an instant, the second you figure out what you want out of life.**

Running on automatic pilot might seem comfortable and easy, but it is the surest road to disaster. There's nothing more useless and wasteful than regret. If the job you have doesn't feel like the right one for you, then figure out what is. To help you uncover your deepest dreams and desires use the PERSONAL AND CA-REER Planner (**www.personalandcareerplanner.com**) to help you get to where you want to be.

Don't ever get caught off-guard

Some days your career wagon rolls along nicely, the horses are eager, the driver's helpful, and the path is smooth. Other times, the road's full of potholes, the driver's a grouch, and the horses refuse to budge.

So as you navigate your career wagon along the road, be absolutely mindful of several things:

1. How's the road ahead of you?

Life can you throw you some surprises, and you would be better off by mitigating risks and taking control of the reins, rather than just going with the flow.

If you're not making deliberate decisions regarding your own career, someone else is already making them for you, although you don't know it. Be on purpose and try not to simply run on automatic pilot. Unless you bring along a map, you just might hit a career dead end. Stop momentarily if you need to catch your breath, but always move forward with a well-defined mission, and a clear destination.

It helps to talk to someone who knows the terrain. In other words, **seek out mentors who can make the road easier** and less painful than it needs to be. You don't have to always pay for your own mistakes in order to learn. Sometimes you can avoid the pain and unnecessary expense by acquiring a few valuable lessons from other people who have walked the same path as you.

If no mentors appear to take you under their wing, then be sure to find one. Whether it's someone outside the company with more experience, a career coach that you have to hire, or even just a good business book where you can get some guidance, make sure that you're taking care of your career.

2. Is your wagon still in good shape?

While you may be working and singing a happy tune, you may not realize that the company you're working for is in debt, under receivership or is about to be split into separate divisions. **Ignorance can be very dangerous to your career.**

Keep your ear to the ground and make sure you're aware of what's happening around you. Your rapid ascent up the corporate ladder might be rudely interrupted if your company goes bankrupt and suddenly has to shut down.

You can, however, be picked up very easily by another employer, if you've made contact with several companies in advance to explore your options. The key is to always have a safety net of alternatives so that you're fully prepared to deal with life's surprises as they occur. And there's going to be many of them.

If the company is not doing well, it may resort to letting go of people in order to survive. **Don't wait to get fired.** Be one step ahead of the game and always be on the lookout for other potential places to work, regardless of how well your company is doing.

If you're constantly nurturing your career, then you don't ever have to be subjected to the various up and down cycles that the economy or your company keeps on going through. You can always ride the top of each wave and always come out ahead of everybody else.

3. Is the driver the same one you started with?

New owners can represent a huge challenge, or opportunity. They may take a shine to you, especially if you're one of the acknowledged performers or veterans, and may even ask for your participation to make the transition smoother. That's the best case scenario.

The worst case scenario with these corporate mergers is when these new owners can sometimes be so intent on completely rewriting the company's organizational chart and bringing in their own trusted lieutenants to replace existing employees. Even with the best intentions, their unfamiliarity with the existing corporate culture may create some friction, and they will most likely impose their own values or ideas that may not sit well with people who have been used to doing things a certain way.

People who have gotten comfortable doing things one way for years may feel alienated by the new culture or boss. If the new management or owners were brought in to turn around an ailing business, you can be sure that things will be totally different once they step on board.

Your whole world could turn upside down. If they don't get along with you, for example, then you're in trouble. You have to try to adjust to the new situation, if you want to keep your job.

4. Is your wagon still on—or off—track?

If you're not being promoted, ask yourself why not? If you can't figure out the answer, have a constructive conversation with your supervisor and find out what you can do to move up. You can reasonably ask for responsibility to match your track record.

Of course that means you have to have a solid record of performance. It's no good going to the boss for a promotion or a raise if you just came off of a bad performance review.

Having the right information before you approach your boss eliminates guesswork and may remove any frustration you may have over being passed over. But if you're not satisfied with the explanation you get, then you can plan your next move, whether it be to stay, move to a different department, or move to a different company altogether.

Don't just accept a bad situation and try to make the best of it. You don't have the time to waste. Start making the necessary changes to get back on track.

5.   Are other wagons trying to pull ahead of you?

Ever come across people who love politics and intrigue and like to feed the rumor mill? They seem to have no better purpose than to polarize your department, make themselves seem more important, and diminish others. People like that cultivate few allies. And you can be sure that they've also picked up some enemies along the way.

Make sure that you steer clear of these people, for two reasons: First, they're wiling to destroy or sabotage other people's projects or their reputations; Second: when they finally get their comeuppance, they sometimes tend to bring other people down with them.

If you're too close to this kind of person, you could fall victim to some of the negative fallout that happens.

Companies sometimes have short memories

If you've been producing hits, make sure to capitalize on them. **Angle for a promotion or a raise while**

you're still in the news, so to speak. Although you'll be patted on the back now, they'll keep on expecting you to keep on hitting those home runs, and in time your goals may turn into a moving target.

If the bar keeps getting higher, it may end up being impossible to jump over one day. Time to consider your next move. There's nothing more frustrating than being given more challenging objectives to hit every year and working longer and longer hours in return for meeting increasing expectations.

You are the superstar of your own career

If you've always wondered about how to be in a charge of a business, you don't have to look very far to find out. You're already managing one: your career.

Let's consider another metaphor: Let's say that you happened to be a new singer. Let's say that you had a very promising start and seemed destined to be the next big thing. But you can't find a good manager, and so you've decided to look after your own musical career.

That means that apart from writing songs and singing them, you have to create CDs, organize world tours to generate sales, pitch one of your songs to ad agencies so they can be used for TV commercials, spin off your own clothing and fragrance lines, create a reality show based on the rise of your career and become a paid endorser for a big shoe or car company.

That would require a lot of work wouldn't it? To extend the metaphor, many of us don't usually write albums and try to generate sales. And we certainly don't go on tour. We don't act as spokespersons for big companies and we don't bother with creating separate streams of income tied to our "brand". We just write songs and sing them.

And many of us complain about how little we make.

- **Publish your "album"**

Your resume is your compilation of hits. Even if you don't plan to move immediately, that document summarizes your achievements within the company. If they're substantial and measurable, you can bring them up with your boss next time you ask for a raise. And you can promote them to other companies, too.

- **Go on "tour"**

Are you active within your industry? Do you get involved with non-profits, or charitable organizations, attend industry events, give presentations to groups within your company or sector? That's how you go on tour. That's when you appear on other employers' radar screens, because they're active in those groups, too.

If you don't find out who your counterparts are in companies within your industry, and make an effort to reach out to them, then you'll stay anonymous and you'll never develop a reputation. If you don't have a reputation, then people won't know who you are and won't be able to recommend you for a better job.

- **Talk to the "promoters"**

Headhunters and recruiters seek out those who establish a higher profile in the industry and develop a reputation as someone who gets things done within their respective companies. These are people who are always in demand.

In his book, "Never Eat Alone" author and consultant Keith Ferrazzi says that "anonymity is death". If no one knows about your product or service, you're not going to survive.

Ever wonder why so many restaurants open and go out of business quickly, many of them quite good ones even? It's because so many of them don't set aside enough money for promotion. In the meantime they have to pay for leases and staff, while waiting for word of mouth to build, which can take years.

You don't want to wait years. No one is going to toot your horn except you. If the idea of drawing attention to yourself makes you uncomfortable, you need to find a way to quietly put yourself forward. It's close to impossible to go up the company ladder or get paid better by staying quietly within your comfort zone. You need to make a bit of noise.

To return to our metaphor, there are probably a lot of talented songwriters and singers that we haven't heard about because they've never understood that marketing, sales and distribution are an integral part of the business of music-making. You can sell out without "selling out." You have to sell out concert venues and sell out your whole inventory of CDs in order to be successful. Selling out isn't necessarily equal to selling out your soul or your artistic integrity.

A word about money

It's true that money isn't everything. **Happiness is what matters to most people.** In one extreme case, millionaire Karl Rabeder of Austria gave away his lakeside villa, his 42-acre farm house in Provence and his business to live a much simpler life. He discovered—after a 3-week holiday in Hawaii with his wife—that his money and possessions weren't giving him peace or joy.

Still, any entrepreneur, artist, architect or contractor, needs to be commercially viable in order to survive and to thrive. They can't churn out work simply to please themselves. Well they can, of course, but they'll be far more successful and happy if other people see the value of their work and are significantly influenced by it.

Picasso and Warhol only became who they were because their audiences enabled them to be famous as a result of hungrily consuming their work, pushing the cost of their paintings to stratospheric levels. Without the validation and permission of their audiences, they would have died unknown and penniless.

Without an approving audience, you can't sell yourself, either. So you have to be aware of the market's tastes and mood at any particular moment. Although you needn't customize your work to fit anybody's preferences, you do have to find the audience that appreciates what you do, and figure out the best way to connect with them.

That kind of business savvy is what separates a Michelangelo from someone similarly talented, but who is struggling to make a living from their profession. Michelangelo was not only skilled technically; he knew how to win commissions from the Pope and from other powerful and influential people of the day.

Some might say he was too good, in fact. His arguably-most-famous work was the Sistine Chapel ceiling, which he never wanted to paint (Michelangelo considered himself a sculptor, after all). However, the strong-willed Pope Julius II was not someone you could just refuse.

In short, although talent matters, the ability to find paying clients and keep them happy and coming back for more is probably more important if one is to not only survive, but thrive in the corporate and business world.

Remember the contractor mindset? It changes everything

When you think of your own career as a business, then you'll view the whole corporate landscape differently. Not only do you view your day to day work differently, but you'll see your employers in a totally new light, as "clients" that you want to please on a daily basis. Don't wait for quarterly reviews. You have to make your client happy at all times, to ensure the continuous "renewal" of your employment contract.

But more importantly, you'll know that the company that you're currently working for isn't the only client around. You'll never again become dependent on one particular employer for career satisfaction, or income. You'll be more attuned to what the competition is charging for their time and expertise, and also be aware of what most employers are willing to pay.

Most importantly, you'll have no hang-ups about ending the relationship and moving on to a different client if you lose motivation or see no further opportunities for growth. You needn't wait for people to give you work, as you'll be constantly looking for work yourself. Conversely, you'll be prepared to land on your feet and get back on the saddle, if ever your company has to let you go for any reason.

Don't leave money on the table

Life doesn't have to be a tradeoff. Although work can be its own reward, there's no reason that you have to be paid poorly for doing what you love. You can certainly do what you love and earn a good income so that you can live the kind of life that you want.

The key to having it all of course, is knowing the going rate. A lot of information can be gained from the internet, a small business assistance center, your industry association, and of course from simply asking people.

Imagine what you would do if you discovered that you should be getting paid thirty thousand dollars more per year. What could you do with that money? Do you think you'd hesitate to ask your boss to correct your salary right away? Don't back away just because it's a difference of "just" two dollars an hour. That's a $4,160 per-year (computed at 40 hours per week times 52 weeks) difference right there.

Companies won't volunteer to pay you more. You have to ask them to do so. And you can't ask them if you don't know what the going rate is. Women, in particular, make about 20 percent less than their male counterparts on their first job out of school according to a study conducted by the American Association of University Women [AAUW]. And many of them aren't even aware of this discrepancy. Knowledge, in this case, really is power. If they're paying you 20 percent less than comparable workers, they're probably willing to meet your demand for a 12 percent raise.

Once you have the facts, you'll be in a better position to find out what to do in order to get paid better. You may need more training, certification, licensing, or a higher level of education. Or perhaps you simply need to ask for more money for yourself.

There's always someone who is willing to pay you better than your current employer. Learn how to use information gathering meetings to see what other more lucrative opportunities are out there at **www.sittingprettycourse.com**

Find out who these companies are and what you need to do, and also who you need to know, to be considered for a position there. And find out what the work entails to see whether it's a good fit for you or not.

You don't have to limit your job search to your own city either. Working abroad can bring you a higher salary too. If you've always dreamed of working someplace exotic, find out which companies are sending their employees abroad for foreign postings. Or you can apply directly to companies that are based in other parts of the world. Oftentimes, you'll be paid better, or your salary will simply go much further, enabling you to save more money or simply enjoy a higher standard of living.

There are definitely tons of exciting opportunities happening in other cities elsewhere. It can be a chance to expand your horizons and meet people who are very different from you. It's your chance to work in a place with a climate that you're not used to, and even to learn an entirely new language or dialect. It would definitely add an interesting chapter to your life and some bonus points to your resume.

CHAPTER 7
BE THE PERSON THAT COMPANIES WANT TO HIRE

Deliver on time and exceed expectations

Complete the tasks assigned to you quickly and efficiently. It's the most basic rule for everyone in the world of work. But if you'd like to get just a single idea out of this entire book that's really useful and lucrative, then it could be this:

You're here to help other people out and make the world a slightly better place using your knowledge and experience.

If you can hang onto that fundamental concept, then you're already ahead of the game. Most people aren't happy with their jobs. Nor are they doing the things they really want to do or causing any significant impact in other peoples' lives. And they're also not aware of, or they're under-utilizing, their special gifts.

They forget that what they do affects everyone else, no matter how insignificant they think their job is. So they do a mediocre job, which in turn affects other people, and creates various negative repercussions in the process.

On the flip side, focusing your mind and purpose on doing some good for other people through your job or business creates a very different impact, and also brings back a tremendously positive outcome for you personally.

Think about it for a second. You are being assigned all these tasks at the office and basically your job is to make sure that these are done properly. But that's just one way of looking at what you're doing. Here are 3 levels at which you can operate:

1. As a performer

At a higher level though, you're also making your boss' and your co-workers' lives a little easier and better as a result of your efforts and your expertise. **If you can establish a reputation as a "go-to" person, or somebody who gets the job done, it will be typically much easier to rise in your profession.** You'll now be known in your workplace, and in your industry, as a performer.

2. As a leader

If you can be relied on to look after things in your boss' absence, then you've established an even higher level of expertise, and moved from performer to leader. What this also does is enable you to see things from the view of the people who run, or may have even founded, the company. You'll be able to see the business through the eyes of an owner who keeps a few people gainfully employed, and has an impact in the community.

3. As an influential resource

If you really want to be noticed, though, and really establish a big reputation throughout your entire community then you can become an advocate or key resource for your company, or even in your industry. Becoming an advocate could also entail heading up your industry association or some nonprofit or civic group like a Rotary Club or your local Chamber of Commerce.

You may even want to write a book about your profession. That involves a bit more effort and more time, of course, but you'll be raising your profile to such a degree that your ideas will be listened to by decision makers at other companies, who will now learn about your existence.

Having this type of experience on your resume gets your name established on a much larger scale. **And when your name and your work ethic precede you, it**

becomes much easier to attract job offers, since people you've never met already know about you.

Decision-makers think that if you can run organizations with large memberships and make solid contributions to these groups, you can easily lead smaller teams of people and meet performance targets assigned to you elsewhere. And when you're a published author or well-known blogger, you'll command even greater respect and awe.

With this kind of reputation, you can charge more for your services since you've created your own track record, and you'll never find yourself wanting for a job since everybody in your industry who needs to know knows who you are, and has a high regard for your abilities.

Develop a reputation for getting things done

Contractors develop a reputation first and foremost as performers. Their reputation lies on their ability to deliver and employers sometimes prefer to work with them due to the fact that they tend to over-deliver and stay later than their employee counterparts. They tend to focus more on work than on politics and are extremely deadline-oriented, typically. Furthermore, they don't watch the clock to see how much time is left to the end of the day.

Contractors don't think of the job simply as a means to an end. The job itself is where they mostly derive satisfaction. They tend to focus on impressing other people on the quality of their work, rather than using superficial markers like attending lots of meetings to impress other people with how hard they seem to be working. Contractors prefer to be measured on the results, not on the amount of face time that they put in at the office.

Although keeping their job or making sure that their contracts are renewed or extended—is a big consideration, it isn't the overriding one. They're already being contacted by various other potential employers even though they're not finished with their current contracts.

Being in demand is a great thing, but it does take some time to establish and it will depend on having a solid grasp of what you do. However, that's really not hard to accomplish provided you're willing to invest the time to develop the necessary expertise in your chosen field.

If your personal style of work is to simply focus on work, and if you can gracefully ignore office politics, then the contractor lifestyle may be for you. It definitely pays more, and you have less of the hassles of normal office life.

If you love doing what you do, then this might be a good option for you, as your rise and fall will depend more on your ability to deliver than your ability to be liked by everyone at the office. Don't go out of your way to annoy people, obviously, but when you're independent, you can take it all with a grain of salt.

Be known as a team player and better yet, organizer

Even in your earliest days in school, one of the things you were evaluated on was your ability to get along and play well with others. The office is no different, although people may show aggressive behavior in more subtle ways. The greater your ability to avoid these destructive types and be able to get people to work together, the greater the chance that more leadership responsibilities will be given to you.

You will be richly rewarded if can sell your ideas, enlist cooperation, and get people moving forward quickly and easily under your direction. **Although working efficiently and producing results is great, the ability to influence other people to work just as hard and deliver results as a focused and coordinated team is even more valuable.**

That's why people who have both the technical and management ability rise to the top faster than employees who just have the technical knowledge. At some point in your career, you usually end up doing more people management than the work you started out doing.

It's not only front line jobs; management and even CEO positions are increasingly being contracted out. If you have an ability to turn around under-performing departments and companies, you can become an executive for hire. And if you can motivate people, fire them up about the company's mission, and keep them happy while doing it, you'll be able to write your own ticket.

Becoming a consultant

- **First, make the mental leap**

The first step to becoming a contractor or consultant is to make a conscious decision to work for yourself and be your own boss. This is the most important step to freedom.

You don't actually have to quit what you're doing now to be self-employed. You can continue working for the same employer. However, an important shift will occur once you make this small, but significant adjustment in your thinking.

Instead of being a "wage slave", you're now a supplier of services, and your company is now suddenly a client. What this does is to prompt you to consider delivering a totally different brand of service, which is less centered on how much you can get out of the company that you're working for, and more focused on what you can do for them, and other similar clients who retain your services.

You'll be playing at a new and higher level, and your motivation to come to work will be completely transformed. Instead of simply trying to keep your job, you'll now be more focused on thinking about ways to improve your performance and that of the company that you're working for, and how you can keep on increasing your expertise to deliver superior service. You might surprise your boss, and even yourself, at how much better you'll be performing.

In fact, you should find yourself becoming more performance-oriented. You'll strip away fear, worry less about your job and constantly prove the value of your services instead. You'll see and feel the results of your involvement immediately. You'll be more motivated to deliver, and you'll have an increased awareness that you now have several "clients" to please: your immediate boss, your department, and the company's own clients.

As a bonus you'll discover more happiness at work, and you'll find greater fulfillment as a result of creating highly satisfied users of your service. Instead of being drained, or in continual, unrelenting competition for a higher spot on the company, you'll be a valuable resource and an important part of the team.

As you free yourself from thinking that you're just another cog in the wheel, you'll come to realize that you can serve other clients, in addition to the one that currently pays your salary. You might even want to consider taking on a second type of client in the same industry, or even a totally different one, on the side.

Or if your present "client" is turning out to be more of a headache than a benefit, you can simply move on to a different client. At this point, you're no longer dependent on one company's approval. You can simply drop your current employer for a new one if it's not working out, or if your job's less than a perfect fit.

Such is the power of being your own boss.

The contractor mindset opens up a whole new range of available positions. One of the most lucrative gigs for proven performers who have just retired or who have left the workforce relatively young (e.g. successful managers who've taken a few years off to raise their families) is to come back to the work force on a limited basis, either as a consultant, or a contract decision-maker with the primary responsibility of creating results for the short term, usually a period less than five years long.

If you don't want to work a full week, or work too long for just one company, this may also prove to be a golden opportunity for you. After all, there's no need to waste all that wisdom and experience when there are newly-founded companies lacking the depth and seasoning that you might provide. You can help their companies develop some solid traction in the market-place. And you can work full-time for just one company for a finite period, or do it part-time for several firms all at once.

There's no need for you to start on the bottom rung again, working at a job with fewer responsibilities, especially after having accumulated years of work experience. A lot in life depends on perception, and if you've positioned your skills and abilities properly, you can sell your time for a higher price.

- **Make the leap on paper**

Once you've decided that you're now a professional provider of services, similar to an accountant or health practitioner, you can take the next step: announcing the presence of your business to the world.

You can begin with the physical: print out business cards and letterheads from your laser printer at home or get them professionally done at your local copy or print shop. You may also want to look into the extremely economical world of online business printers, who deal in bulk.

So now, when you're at a networking event or even just casually socializing with other people, you'll have a credible, professional business card with the name of your firm (you can start by using your surname, e.g. "Smith Consulting Group") and your contact information to hand out.

You should also start thinking about a brief info-mercial outlining what you do and what types of clients you'd like to work with. Your infomercial isn't for broadcast. It's simply a capsule explanation in layperson's terms that you'll use to explain what you do at social or networking events.

Once you meet and talk to other consultants out there, you'll discover that they don't talk in terms of who they work for at all. They never say "I work for ABC company". They'll always talk about what they do and how they do it. And so should you.

The reason for this is that they have a contractor mentality: They're fully aware that they're in a temporary situation, and that they can expect to change clients often, so it doesn't matter who they're working for just now.

So instead of announcing that you work at so-and-so accounting corporation, architecture firm, or pharmaceutical company you can say that you "provide financial services", or "design beautiful and functional homes for people" or "help maintain people's health and well-being."

What you may not realize is that you're also announcing your work mission; your means of changing the world through the company that you work with. The company is simply the primary vehicle for delivering your unique brand of service.

Whether you're a Vice-president or an assistant, keep in mind that your job is as critical as anyone else's.

If you can't believe that, then you'll never understand the full potential of your job. Why else would you go to a place for forty hours a week, if it weren't that important? Think of your salary not as the reason for being at work, but rather as validation for a job well done.

Anybody can call themselves a contractor or consultant, and most people take it at face value. The important thing, though, is to believe it yourself. Once you create a line that mentally separates you from your firm, and make the transition from employee to independent supplier of services, then you'll be truly on your way to career freedom.

- **Make the leap in the real world**

Once you're ready to make the big leap to freedom and have all your marketing collateral ready, you need to choose:

On one hand, you can close your eyes, take a big leap into the unknown, and work on developing your new consulting business full-time. On the other, you can take the smaller step of establishing your client base, while continuing to work from your current employer's office as you make your transition.

The first few years may be a bit uneven. You may have periods when you're really busy, and also times when you won't be, so having a cushion of six months' to a year's worth of salary in savings will help to move you past slow periods and the occasional feelings of uncertainty and self-doubt that you'll be sure to face while you're establishing your professional practice.

As an independent contractor, you'll have to keep your pipeline filled with potential clients or prospects to serve. The first and best way to make sure that you're in demand is to deliver good service and exceed client expectations.

Secondly, you'll need to get your name out there either by building your client list one person at a time, or by the more passive and high-tech approach of attracting traffic to your website and converting these visitors to paying clients in the real world.

For more specific information on how to build your new consulting business, and gain greater financial independence and freedom, go to **www.fromwageslavetoselfemployed.com**

Be the person that no one says anything negative about

Contractors may or may not be touched by corporate politics, but they usually never have to be involved in them. They're not preoccupied with having to maintain appearances in order to keep their jobs; they already know that each day could be their last, and therefore they're primarily engaged in completing the task at hand rather than playing exhausting mind games.

That said, they also try to handle people with great respect. What comes out of your mouth can come back to bite you, so be careful about saying things that might be taken out of context. If anything try to stay neutral while the battle rages around you. Be completely solid and reliable and don't spill sensitive information that you've been given.

You need to cultivate a laissez faire attitude about loose remarks and office gossip, and simply shrug your shoulders when someone tries to pass on "juicy" information to you. Intrigues may be a "normal" part of the office life, but it's a particularly dangerous vortex that does nothing toward keeping you continuously employed. Keep your ear to the ground by all means. Just don't talk about what you hear.

Such a strategy won't make you really popular with any one group of people, but on the other hand keeping a fairly low profile is fine. And sometimes being seen as a neutral party with no discernable allegiance is all it takes to remain employed.

You still should try and shine through your work, but an even temperament and ability to get along are part of your basic tool kit. People who can tread the straight and narrow while others are dipping into the gutter of rumor and innuendo are always in demand, and never fear for their jobs.

Keep work coming through the door by developing a solid network

Being the "go to" person in your industry doesn't happen by accident. This takes some work on your part. Friendships don't thrive on their own. Sure, you shared good times in high school, but the relationship has to evolve beyond that as this period of your life becomes a fading memory. Otherwise these friendships will fade too.

Likewise, clients don't automatically become repeat buyers of your services just because of one good experience with you. You have to remind them that you exist throughout the year. Since people aren't thinking about you all the time, even though the need may arise for your type of service, you might not get the call unless you're keeping up the contact.

If you fail to stay in touch, you'll fall off their radar screens pretty easily. In business, ensuring that you have people's attention is called "maintaining top of mind awareness" and that's a very valuable thing to nurture, especially if you want to have repeat business.

If there's just one thing that can easily set you apart from your peers, then it's this: Never forget to keep in touch with people you've worked with in the past, especially your former supervisor or even people above your old boss, if you ever managed to develop a solid relationship with that person. Most people totally miss out on the opportunity to develop a solid network just by failing to keep in touch.

Never forget that people that you've worked with during the early stage of your career and who have stayed behind may eventually rise up the corporate ladder, or they may be hired by other companies you want to work—or do business—with.

If you've let the relationship cool off, then you're losing out. And if you've gone into business for yourself, you should take your friends off the back burner and call them up. You're not trolling for work. Just keeping in touch and seeing if there's anything you can do for them.

Fortunately, it's pretty easy to keep in touch with the people from the start of your career. Just use important occasions throughout the year such as major holidays, or their birthdays (assuming you know the date) to give them a call or send an email or card. Often that's enough to keep the relationship going, and it will pave the way for you to help each other, not just in business but in general.

Here's a two minute exercise: Think of a friend you met professionally but haven't talked to in a while: Pick up the phone and call them (preferably when you know they aren't busy). When they answer, say "Hey. We haven't talked in a while and I just wondered how you were getting on."

Let them do most of the talking. At the end of that call, the person on the other end is probably thinking that it was nice of you to touch base. And if a position opens up that's in your area of expertise, then guess whose name that person will have in mind?

Establish yourself as an expert

You'll also get better paid by positioning yourself an expert in your chosen field. If you're still thinking of yourself as a graphic designer, policeman, or whatever your job is, then you haven't fully understood the potential behind what you do. Whether you're working for yourself or somebody else, your work involves a lot more than simply delivering your product or service. That's only part of what you do. What you are is a problem-solver and a valuable resource.

It's time to think of yourself as one of the foremost experts in your chosen field—Someone people seek out to make their own lives better and richer.

If you're passionate about what you're doing, and you think the world will truly benefit if they buy your product or service, then it shouldn't be a problem for you to talk to people passionately about how you can make their lives better as a result of your knowledge and experience. If public speaking makes you break out into a cold sweat, go to the internet first. Just about anyone with any expertise has a blog.

Before Julie Powell came out with her first book, "Julie & Julia," she wrote a daily blog about her experiences cooking all 524 of Julia Child's recipes from the latter's bestselling book "Mastering the Art of French Cooking" in one year. The blog eventually developed a loyal fan base and attracted the interest of literary agents and television producers.

Powell's blog was eventually turned into a book, and caught the attention of Nora Ephron, the famous screenwriter of romantic hit movies such as "When Harry Met Sally" and "Sleepless in Seattle".

With Ephron's participation, "Julie & Julia" was made into a movie starring Meryl Streep and Amy Adams in 2009. Powell has since written another book called "Cleaving: Marriage, Meat and Obsession".

With modern publishing resources, the book is becoming the 21st century's new business card. If you haven't thought about writing one, then you should. It's your best bet to achieving respectability in your chosen field and your ticket to international recognition and financial independence. But start off by writing a blog or newsletter first. Work out what's interesting to you and to your readers. The book can come later once you're ready.

As long as your thoughts resonate with people, then it's possible to build an audience of hundreds of thousands of people for your blog in a very short amount of time. The information that you have to share may not be ground-breaking, but what will make you interesting is your own expert point of view.

And if you really know your stuff, can write decently, and are willing to share a little insight, then you can achieve expert recognition before you have to come out on TV or on the radio to do interviews related to your expertise. By taking baby steps such as putting together a blog, or a newsletter, you can work toward larger audiences.

That's why new travel books come out every day, for example, even though there are thousands already out there. There are endless ways to provide fresh perspective. It's like revisiting a favorite destination at different points in your life. You tend to have a whole new experience each time because you're constantly evolving, and therefore look at the same places differently each time.

You'll find that a lot of people will always want to read about articles that are in their field of interest, although they may have come across similar ones before. And they will eventually find you and may want to keep updated with your most recent thoughts and experiences, since these are more or less in alignment with theirs. And once you have an audience there's another potentially lucrative activity that you should consider: giving talks. If you're a recognized authority, that can pay money, too.

President Bill Clinton's speaking fee is apparently as high as $425,000 for an hour-long speech. We can't all be Clinton, but would you give a speech for a thousand dollars? How about five thousand dollars?

If the mere thought of it makes you want to faint, then there are other channels you can explore, such as writing books or audio talks. Being a good speaker just takes practice. If you speak in front of an audience of just 10 people several times, then speaking in front of an audience of a hundred people becomes less of a big deal.

If shyness is a real problem for you, there are a number of groups out there, such as Business Network International or BNI (www.bni.com) and Toastmasters (www.toastmasters.org) that can help you develop your confidence. Members take on active leadership roles and learn how to make proper introductions, make elevator speeches (essentially a 60-second infomercial), how to make small talk (incredibly difficult for many people, believe it or not), and how to give (and ask for) business.

Build credibility with yourself

If you're willing to look at your job in a completely new light and you're ready to think like a contractor, you'll have run into this question: **"Why would people listen to me? And what will I say if I get asked a question that I don't know the answer to?"**

You're setting yourself up as a professional, an expert. Surely you should have all the answers? Well, it turns out that even though we each know a lot, we don't know all the answers to questions about our business. If you're caught short, you can always say that you'll get back to the person with the answer. Your candor will be appreciated by your clients. **An expert doesn't carry all the facts in his or her head. But he or she will know where to find them.**

It's your experience that makes you an expert. Don't let anyone tell you differently. And you don't need a PhD or a decade of experience to speak to an audience, work on a project or do a particular type of job as long as you genuinely love and deeply believe in what you're doing. With the right attitude, the learning comes easily.

A lot of people overcome their fear of public speaking simply as a result of their eagerness to share the benefits of what they do to anyone that will listen. If you're a true believer in your own product or service, you'll never have to try and "convince" anyone ever again of anything. People will catch your enthusiasm and conviction and take you at your word.

Whether you do it by being an invaluable resource for your industry or by publishing your thoughts online or in print, you can certainly solidify your reputation, and get a guaranteed income for life by being the expert in your field, and employing the contractor mindset.

To find out how to build your career as an expert and attract the attention of employers almost effortlessly instead of having to go out and chase them, go to **www.sittingprettycourse.com**

Visit the author's website at **www.georgeverdolaga.com** to discover:

- *Tips and techniques to develop a highly stable career that will make worrying about getting fired or down-sized a thing of the past*

- *Valuable insights to on how to continuously bring value to the workplace and be highly regarded by your bosses and co-workers*

- *How to stand out from a crowded sea of job applicants in a sluggish economy, a small town, or even a new city that you've just moved to where you don't know a single soul*

- *Why knowing yourself inside and out is part of the formula for being successful, and also making a meaningful contribution to the world*

- *Practical ways to overcome your fears and inhibitions so that you can share your message and influence people.*

- *The path to becoming a valued and respected resource in your particular field, and how to be paid well for the privilege*

- *How to get out of your own way, achieve your goals with the help of other people and be happy*

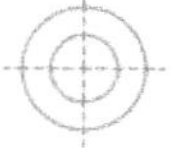 VERDOLAGA LEARNING SYSTEMS

REFERENCES

"AAUW's Position on Pay Equity." AAUW. <http://www.aauw.org/advocacy/issue_advocacy/actionpages/paye quity.cfm>

"Accenture To Lay Off Senior Exec Staff By 7%." August 21, 2009. Business Standard News. <http://www.business-standard.com/india/news/accenture-to-lay-off-senior-exec-staff-by-7/12/46/71347/on>

"Americans Hate Their Jobs More Than Ever: Satisfaction Level Hits New Low, Especially Among Younger Workers." 26 February 2007. Livescience.com.< http://www.msnbc.msn.com/id/17348695>

Archibald, Dale. "Our ever-expanding work week." 1997. Gary Johnson's Brave New Work World NewWork News. <http://www.newwork.com/Pages/Opinion/Archibald/Work%20W eek.html>

Baker, Peter. "Bill Clinton To Name Donors As Part Of Obama Deal." 29 November 2008. New York Times. <http://www.nytimes.com/2008/11/30/washington/30clinton.html>

Blanchard, Ken and Spencer Johnson. The One Minute Manager. New York: William Morrow and Company, 1982.

Bortz, Abe. "Historical Development of the Social Security Act." Posted 26 Feb 2010. Social Security Online. <http://www.ssa.gov/history/bortz.html>

"Building a Lattice Organization." 02 December 2008. Deloitte.com. <http://www.deloitte.com/view/en_US/us/Services/additional-services/mass-career-customiza-

tion/article/e41a7e74622fb110VgnVCM100000ba42f00aRCRD.ht
m>

Canfield, Jack and Janet Switzer. The Success Principles: How To
Get From Where You Are To Where You Want To Be. New York :
William Morrow and Company, 2004.

Caryn-Rabin, Roni."Teen Smoking Rates Decline." 15 December
2008.   New   York   Times.
<http://www.nytimes.com/2008/12/16/health/research/16smoking.
html>

"Child labor in factories: A new workforce during the Industrial
Revolution."   2002.   Needham   High   School.
<http://nhs.needham.k12.ma.us//cur/Baker_00/2002_p7/ak_p7/chil
dlabor.html>

Chopra, Deepak. Ageless Body. Timeless Mind: The Quantum
Alternative to Growing Old. New York: Random House, 1993.

"Cigarette Ads Target Youth, Violating $250 Billion 1998
Settlement." 12 March 2002. The University of Chicago Medical
Center.   <http://www.uchospitals.edu/news/2002/20020312-
tobacco.html>

"CityTV Lays Off Staff In News Division." 19 January 2010.
CBC   News.
<http://www.cbc.ca/arts/media/story/2010/01/19/citytv-
layoffs.html>

Cohen, Marcy. "The Privatization of Health Care Cleaning
Services in Southwestern British Columbia, Canada" 28 February
2002.   Wiley   Interscience   Journal.
<http://www3.interscience.wiley.com/journal/118562160/abstract?
CRETRY=1&SRETRY=0>

Conachy, James. "Mass Layoffs Underway In Japan." 27 August 2001. World Socialist Web Site. <http://www.wsws.org/articles/2001/aug2001/jap-a27.shtml>

Covey, Stephen. The 7 Habits of Highly Effective People: Powerful Lessons in Personal Change. New York: Simon and Schuster, 1989.

Cullen, Lisa. "Three Signs Of A Miserable Job." 21 August 2007. Time.com. <http://workinprogress.blogs.time.com/2007/08/21/three_signs_of_a_miserable_job/>

"Cultural Categories." USAID Community Connections. <http://www.ccfrussia.ru/?mod=s_page&sp_id=336>

Dickler, Jessica. "More Work, Same Pay." 5 June 2009. CNNMoney.com. <http://money.cnn.com/2009/06/03/news/economy/more_work/index.htm>

Dodge, John. "First Comes Hydrogen Cars: The Refueling Infrastructure Will Follow." 11 August 2008. Design News. <http://www.designnews.com/article/47462-First_Comes_Hydrogen_Cars.php>

Dumpala, Preethi. "The Year The Newspaper Died." 4 July 2009. BusinessInsider.com. <http://www.businessinsider.com/the-death-of-the-american-newspaper-2009-7>

Dunkin, Amy. "The Ladder Is Out, The Lattice Is In." 24 October 2007. BusinessWeek.com. <http://www.businessweek.com/careers/workingparents/blog/archives/2007/10/as_you_may_have.html>

"Employee Tenure Summary." 26 September 2008. Bureau of Labor Statistics Economic News Release. <http://www.bls.gov/news.release/tenure.nr0.htm>

Ferrazzi, Keith. Never Eat Alone. New York: Currency Doubleday, 2005.

Fitchard, Kevin. "Bell Canada Tests MPLS In Life-And-Death Application." Connected Planet. 10 Mar 2003. <http://connectedplanetonline.com/broadband/print/telecom_bell_c anada_tests/>

Hensley, Russell et al. "Electrifying Cars: How Three Industries Will Evolve. " June 2009. Climate Change Special Initiative / McKinsey Quarterly. <http://www.mckinseyquarterly.com/Energy_Resources_Materials /Strategy_Analysis/Electrifying_cars_How_three_industries_will_ evolve_2370>

Horton, Leslie. "Stress Reduction." Mind Body Medicine. <http://www.mindbodymedicine.ca/stress_reduction.html>

Johnson, Spencer. Who Moved My Cheese: An Amazing Way to Deal with Change in Your Work and in Your Life. New York: GP Putnam and Sons, 1998.

Keegan, Paul. "Laid Off At 50: What Next?" 11 December 2008. CNN Money. <http://money.cnn.com/2008/12/08/pf/laidoff_atfifty.moneymag/in dex.htm>

Koeppel, David. "Thousands Losing Jobs In Housing Crisis." 22 Sep 2008. MSN Money.

<http://articles.moneycentral.msn.com/Investing/StockInvestingTr ading/thousands-losing-jobs-in-housing-crisis.aspx>

"Loving The Job You Hate: Tips To Make Things Better In A Position That Doesn't Rouse Your Interest." 7 December 2005. Forbes.com. <http://www.msnbc.msn.com/id/10372274>

McKay, Harvey. Dig your Well Before You're Thirsty. New York: Doubleday, 1997.

Montagna, Joseph. "The Industrial Revolution." Posted 21 Feb 2010. Yale-New Haven Teachers Institute. <http://www.yale.edu/ynhti/curriculum/units/1981/2/81.02.06.x.html>

Ohsten, Frederik. "A Left Turn In Japan." 28 August 2009. In Defence Of Marxism. <http://www.marxist.com/left-turn-in-japan.htm>

"Privatization Deal Slashes Hospital Cleaning." Feb 25, 2008. CUPE. <http://cupe.ca/privwatchfeb08/Privatization_deal_s>

Peters, Tom and Robert Waterman. In Search of Excellence: Lessons from America's Best Run Companies. New York: Harper and Row, 1982.

"Recessions And Recoveries.(World Economic History)(Statistical Data Included)." World Economic Outlook. 01 April 2002. <http://goliath.ecnext.com/coms2/gi_0199-1836019/Recessions-and-recoveries.html>

Robbins, Tony. Awaken the Giant Within: How to Take Immediate Control of Your Mental, Emotional, Physical and Financial Destiny. New York: Fireside Books, 1994.

Rogacion, Rosanna. "The Mind-Body Connection: Unresolved Emotional Issues Can Cause Disease." 18 September 2007. Suite101.com. <http://chronicillness.suite101.com/article.cfm/the_mindbody_connection>

Rosenberg-McKay, Dawn. "How Often Do People Change Careers?" 28 July 2006. About.com. <http://careerplanning.about.com/b/2006/07/28/how-often-do-people-change-careers.htm>

Ross-Sorkin, Andrew and Vikas Bajaj. "Shift for Goldman and Morgan Marks the End of an Era." 21 September 2008. New York Times. <http://www.nytimes.com/2008/09/22/business/22bank.html>

Shen, Fern. "Bloodbath Tallied: 40 Baltimore Sun Newsroom Employees Laid Off." Apr 29, 2009. Baltimore Brew. <http://baltimorebrew.com/blog/2009/04/29/yesterdays-bloodbath-tallied-40-baltimore-sun-newsroom-employees-laid-off-union-says/>

Snyder, Chris. "Circuit City to Close 155 Stores, Lay Off Thousands." 3 November 2008 Wired.com. <http://www.wired.com/epicenter/2008/11/circuit-city-to/>

Stone, Irving. The Agony and the Ecstasy: A Biographical Novel Of Michelangelo. New York: Doubleday, 1961.

Sunkle-Pierucki, Linda. "Reassessing The Value Of Blue Collar Labor In A White Collar-Obsessed World." 26 Feb 2010. Helium. <http://www.helium.com/items/1207023-the-practical-skills-of-blue-collar-workers>

Trower, Cathy. "Traditionalists, Boomers, Xers And Millenials: Giving And Getting The Mentoring You Want." 16 October 2009. Brown University. <http://www.brown.edu/Administration/Provost/Advance/Trower%20Generations%20and%20Mentoring.ppsx>

Tuttle, Carolyn. "Child Labor during the British Industrial Revolution." edited by Robert Whaples. August 14, 2001. Lake Forest College. <http://eh.net/encyclopedia/article/tuttle.labor.child.britain>

"United States Recession History." Recession.org. http://recession.org/history

"Western Bankers Head East Amid Sub-Prime Crisis: Report ." 21 April 2008. Barclays News. <http://www.thaindian.com/newsportal/world-news/western-bankers-head-east-amid-sub-prime-crisis-report_10040415.html#ixzz0h9oAKQPu>

"White-Collar Worker." Absolute Astronomy. 7 Feb 2010. <http://absoluteastronomy.com/topics/White-collar_worker>

"Whys and Wherefores: An Introductory Manual for Members Of Boards Of Trustees And Advisory Councils." Scripps Gerontology Center, Miami University. <http://www.cas.muohio.edu/n4a/Origins%20of%20Social%20Security%20(more).htm>

Woolley, Pieta. "Low Wages Hammer Families." 3 Apr 2008. The Georgia Straight. <http://www.straight.com/article-139281/low-wages-hammer-families

INDEX

ABOUT THE AUTHOR

George Verdolaga is the founder and president of Flowform Design Group, an interior design consulting and project management firm based in Vancouver, British Columbia.

His work has been featured in the Vancouver Sun, Real Living, Metro Home and Entertaining and Spectacular Homes of Western Canada.

Teaching and helping people get out of their own way and move closer to their desired outcomes are two of his greatest passions.

Before getting into the interior designer business, George worked for eleven years as the administrator, teacher and education program advisor for the Westdrive Educational Foundation (WEF).

For the past eight years, he has been active in his local church's Sunday school, or Parish Religious Education Program (PREP), as a Grade three teacher.

During his 22 years in the workforce, he has been on both sides of the fence as an employee and business owner. Along the way, he has discovered the simple and effective secrets to attracting employers who have become loyal lifetime fans.

He and his wife currently work as independent contractors.

Go to **www.resumetoolkit.com** to learn the right way to present your credentials and experience on paper:

- ***Find out how to write a strong resume*** *that will attract maximum interest and enable you to get more callbacks*

- ***Discover how to create a cover letter with big impact*** *to enable you to land that critical first meeting*

- ***Understand how to write a powerful thank-you letter*** *that can help potential employers reconsider you for a job even after you've been rejected for a position that is a good fit*

- ***Learn how use these three elements to get work,*** *even if you're new in town or applying for a job with very little experience*